# BUILDING THE AGRICULTURAL CITY

OTHER WORKS BY ROBERT WOLF

Nonfiction
*In Search of America*
*The Triumph of Technique*
*The Writer Within: A Complete and Enjoyable Guide to Writing
    from Everyday Life*
*Crazeology: The Jazz Life of Bud Freeman*
*Story Jazz: A History of Chicago Jazz Styles*
*An American Mosaic: Prose and Poetry by Everyday Folk*
*Heartland Portrait: Stories and Essays from the Rural Midwest*

Fiction
*Grand Tally: A True Account of Recent Events in Moosehead,
    Montana and New York City*

Plays
*Driftless Dreams: A Play for Voices*
*Ragnarok: The Doom of the Gods*
*In Search of America*
*Lucrezia: A History that Never Happened*
*The Austringer*
*Edward the Confessor*
*The Strike at Pullman*
*Heartland Portrait*
*The Diplomat*
*The Special Prosecutor (with Wayne Julin)*

Film
*Regionalism: An Idea Whose Time Has Come*

# BUILDING THE AGRICULTURAL CITY

By
Robert Wolf

Ruskin Press
Decorah, Iowa

First edition. ISBN: 978-0-9741826-4-3

# ACKNOWLEDGMENTS

Publication of Building the Agricultural City was made possible by donations from Eva Theiler, Murray Hudson, Bruce Carlson, Julie Fisher, Kate Gilbert, Rod Haynes, Margaret & Robert Gilbert, William & Susan Hogan, Alice Swenson, Robert Karp, Daryl & Norma Jean Bosma, Alan Lerstrum, Roger & Joyce Isaacs, Craig Hultgren, Phillip & Monique Hooker, Anne Bailey, Tabita Green, Barbara Massman, Bruce Jordan, Judy Goldberg and Thayer Caerter.

Earlier versions of "Provincial Hope," appeared in American Mosaic, published by Oxford University Press, and in The New Regionalism, published by Ice Cube Press. "Building the Agricultural City" is a revision of "On Developing Rural Regional Economies," which was written as a six-part radio editorial for Iowa Public Radio. It was subsequently published in American Mosaic and reprinted in *The Des Moines Register.* "Whose Game Do We Play? Theirs or Ours?" Originally appeared in an on-line news magazine published by Stay Thirsty Media.

I wish to thank Julie Fischer, Elisabeth Rosales, and Bonnie Koloc, my wife, for proofreading the manuscript. Julie's enthusiastic support of the book and the larger economic development project kept me on track. I owe a debt of thanks to H. George Anderson for reading the manuscript and raising questions, and to Jon Andelson for reading and commenting on Part One. Dusty Sang, publisher of Stay Thirsty Media, has always believed in this project and its goals, and has been a valued voice. Thanks also to Michael Espey and Kirby Olson for making a video to promote the book.

## NOTE

Part One of *Building the Agricultural City* is polemical and describes the constraints that must be faced in the design of a self-reliant economy. Part Two focuses on the design process and the tools that can increase regional self-sufficiency. The model civilization that is proposed can be constructed in any region small enough for its people to have a common identity sufficient to encourage collaboration.

# TABLE OF CONTENTS

# PROLOGUE

*The Driftless Region*

I am standing on a ridge in the Driftless region of the American Midwest. From this ridge I can see land rolling to the horizon for miles around.

This is farmland, and the hills are dotted every quarter of a mile with a cluster of buildings—a barn, a silo, a white house. Each spring the earth is plowed into contoured strips that follow the curve of the hills. The fields are lined with hedgerows that provide shelter and habitat for rabbits, pheasants and a dozen more birds and small mammals.

It is now high summer. The contoured strips are covered with alternating strips of yellow corn and green alfalfa. Above, on the blue sky, drift puffs of clouds.

The Driftless is a region, roughly the size of Massachusetts, covering parts of four contiguous states cut through by the Mississippi: Iowa, Minnesota, Wisconsin, and Illinois. It is a land of rolling hills and winding valleys. The land sings, it is beautiful, and seeing it from this ridge I can believe that I live within a great garden tended by farmers.

A hundred and fifty-some years ago this was a self-reliant and largely self-sufficient region. Its people, separated by great distances from the centers of production, needed to supply their own food and goods. They could not wait for flour to be shipped from Chicago or lumber from Eau Claire. They needed to manufacture their own clothes, mill their own lumber, wool, and flour. To take but one example, in 1880 the four northeastern-most Iowa counties had a total of 80 mills—gristmills, woolen mills, lumber mills. Today, in 2016, there are none.

When clam beds were discovered in the Upper Mississippi in the late nineteenth century, clamming became a major industry in Driftless river towns. Button factories were established in several, including Lansing, Iowa and Prairie du Chien, Wisconsin. There blanks were cut from shells and buttons made from the blanks. Twenty thousand men were said to be clamming on the Mississippi and its tributaries in the summer of 1902. Even more men came the next spring, but the beds had been over harvested and the take was considerably smaller. From then on, the industry declined, and commercial fishing took its place.

Carp and buffalo were the main species of commercial fish, and each year, thousands of pounds of carp were put on ice and shipped by freight train to New York for the Jewish market. Before commercial fishing, almost everyone fished. Mr. Henry Canfield of La Crosse told one writer that "All river folks, including boatmen, lumberjacks, raftsmen, adjacent farmers, and nearby townsmen, caught and used fish in quantities. Fish were plentiful all along the rivers."

Houses, mills, retail stores and banks were built from local lumber or from limestone blocks quarried here in the Driftless.

People made and raised what they could. Farm women tended gardens and canned vegetables and meat. They made dresses from flour sacks. Towns people and river people, without radios, televisions, movies and records, held dances where they made their own music.

Today country dances, even town dances with home-made music are a rarity. Few people raise vegetables and fewer can or freeze them. Aside from a handful of commercial fishermen, the fishing industry is gone, along with the clamming and button industry and mills. The region has few manufacturing plants and imports most of its food and goods. Agribusiness aside, the Driftless is a service economy, which accounts for its poverty and the out-migration of its youth.

A century ago, every eight or so miles along the highways that crisscross this land of farmsteads lay a village of one hundred or a thousand folk. Since the mechanization of farming and the consequent dwindling of farm numbers, many hamlets have shriveled or disappeared. The towns that survive are now usually about sixteen miles apart. *Still, this is agrarian society at its best. Its members aid one another in times of illness or disaster.* When someone here is ravaged by cancer and has not the money for surgery and treatment, auctions are held and collections taken up.

When a tornado came through one year and took down a giant Norwegian pine that landed alongside the back of our house, knocked down a chimney and tore up our roof, and then moved a quarter mile and flattened a neighbor's barn, nearby farmers arrived at the farm 2 a.m. with chainsaws and skid loaders to cut through beams and release trapped and wounded animals. The next morning three of those farmers came to our house and cut the fallen pine into logs and rounds and loaded them onto pickups and hauled them off.

Their fathers had worked the same land and had lived and worked cooperatively: the men with threshing and woodcutting, the women with quilt making. This is the image of this region at its most welcoming. But as everyone who has driven through the region knows, many of its towns are rife with empty storefronts. Farm auction notices are posted on café bulletin boards. Villages and towns that once boasted a Saturday night band concert in the town square while farm families shopped and socialized are nearly lifeless.

Many people hope to revitalize their towns by proposing bike trails, or the Main Street program, or something else, but are frequently opposed by a chorus of townsfolk who want "to keep things the way they are." This, of course, is a recipe for further decline. When stores close and school enrollment dwindles, that is change. And while the conservative townsfolk ruefully acknowledge this change, they very often oppose the remedial solutions which have been effective elsewhere. Can anything be done?

*The Agricultural City*
The title for this book was inspired by the phrase "agricultural city," coined by Chicago architect Joe Lambke. Joe used the phrase in the title of a pamphlet which described his vision of a possible future for northeast Iowa. *In Joe's vision, the towns and villages of this four-county rural area in northeast Iowa would be considered nodes of population within one unit—an agricultural city. Unlike the cities we habitually envision, this one would be comprised primarily of farmland, with agriculture the glue that bound cities, villages, towns and farms together.*

I learned about Joe in the early 1990s when I was pondering the problem of rural economic development. I discussed it with Bill Burke, the city planner for Waukon, Iowa, and told him of my own vision for regional development. Bill then mentioned Joe and told me that Joe had submitted a proposal to ten northeast Iowa towns for cooperative economic development. He gave me a copy of the proposal.

I called Joe and we met several times in Chicago and in northeast Iowa, but eventually we lost touch. Joe went on to design furniture and buildings, but the notion of an agricultural city stayed with me, and in 1994 I wrote a six-part editorial for Iowa Public Radio, "Developing Regional, Rural Economies." This won the Sigma Delta Chi Award and Bronze Medal from the Society of Professional Journalists for Best Radio Editorial of the year. The *Des Moines Register* reprinted it one Sunday for their lead editorial, and that, as far as the public was concerned, was pretty much the end of it.

But I continued pondering how a cluster of cities might collaborate; my ideas are sketched in chapter one of Part Two. Here suffice it to say that I envisioned several Agricultural Cities in Iowa, in Wisconsin, and in Minnesota, but only one in the small portion of northwest Illinois that is in the Driftless.

For the next decade I continued to write and publish essays on regionalism and conducted and published two multi-county regional surveys. But none of these efforts attracted more notice than a corpse in a funeral home.

*The End of a World*
Lewis Mumford coined the apt phrase "Power Complex," indicating the convergent forces in government, industry, finance, and military that control our society. But the Power Complex, as increasing numbers of people see, is in its last years, and unless sufficient numbers of people can agree on what a sustainable culture might look like, and begin working to achieve it, chaos and violence will follow the approaching collapse.

The desire for unlimited control, which is the goal of the Power Complex, is a telling instance of rigidity: it is persistent and undeviating. It has an autonomous life, for as one set of leaders retires or dies, another set—a virtual carbon copy—replaces it. The Power Complex is rigid in its dogma of free trade and unrestrained competition. Everyone everywhere must see things as it does. If not, it will force compliance, as John Perkins testified in *Confessions of an Economic Hit Man*. A healthy society is defined in part by its ability to take self-corrective measures; whereas dogmatism and the desire for total control are forms of rigidity, and rigidity is a sign of death.

Conversely, flexibility and adaptability are signs of life and health. As the seventy-sixth verse of the *Tao Teh Ching* says, "When living, man is supple and yielding; when dead, man is hard and stiff. When living, all animals and plants are soft and pliant; when dead, they are withered and brittle. Thus, being inflexible and unyielding is part of dying; being flexible and yielding is part of living." Like a belief system before it dies, a civilization rigidifies as it atrophies: dominant beliefs become dogma, and the civilization becomes incapable of adapting to change, incapable of self-corrective, rectifying measures.

*Regionalism and Possibility*
A new world, now in embryo, is struggling to be born. Human scale communities and human scale sustainable institutions are arising around the planet, and they are arising in reaction to the inhumanity and self-destructive tendencies of the present system.

As of this writing small community discussion groups on various facets of community sustainability are meeting regularly in cities as well as rural towns. People across the country from all walks of life now share an increased sense of the urgent need to build local and regional economies. They may seldom articulate exactly what needs doing, but they know that our present system is collapsing.

Over the past few years increasing numbers of people have been promoting local food systems, local energy production, and community development banks as means by which to restrict the reach of transnational corporations and large urban banks into every corner of our economic and cultural life. These tools are understood to be a means by which to retain more dollars within local economies. Now what some people are coming to realize is that local strategies for economic sustainability can be applied on a regional level.

*Sections, Regions and Bioregions*
Once upon a time the United States was a quiltwork of distinct re-

gions. For example, Colonial New England's democratic character was shaped by its Congregational churches, in which the congregants of each church formed that church's governing body. The churches also served as town meeting halls, where local affairs were decided. The coastal South, on the other hand, settled by Anglicans, was hardly as democratic. Both the Chesapeake Bay and Carolina coastal regions were hierarchical, with slaves at the bottom and wealthy planters at the top and yeomen farmers and poor whites in between.

Large-scale, easy-to-spot distinctions between Colonial New England and the coastal South are as clear as the differences between each of them contrasted with the Middle West frontier or the Spanish Southwest. The regionalization of the United States exists now only as an imaginative possibility, but for several hundred years it existed in fact.

Regions lack strict definition since they are creations of natural forces and therefore lack definite boundaries. Regions blend into one another, in imperceptible degrees, as the agricultural land of the Midwest prairie yields to the Great Plains, and the plains in turn are transformed into desert. Within the last few decades, regions have been defined most commonly in terms of their geology and topography, their watersheds, their flora and fauna. When viewed in this perspective, Maine has more in common with Canada's maritime provinces (New Brunswick, Nova Scotia, and Newfoundland) than with other New England states, while northern California, Oregon, Washington, and British Columbia share more features with each other than with their neighboring states and provinces. In fact, these Pacific Northwest entities are the subject of a pro-business separatist movement that would like to see them form into the independent nation of Cascadia.

The idea of an independent nation in the Northwest originated with Thomas Jefferson, who envisioned the "Republic of the Pacific." According to one anonymous internet source, one of the goals of "'The Pacific Northwest Economic Region' is to build a world class workforce to make the Pacific Northwest economic region competitive in worldwide markets . . ."

*This view of regionalism is called bioregionalism, and I contend that harnessing the idea of a bioregion with the strategies of local economics is our only effective counter to globalization and the collapse of our economic system.*

## Centralization versus Decentralization

Some degree of centralization is needed to implement the most basic functions of a national economy and government. The United States, however, has concentrated finance and business in so few hands that studies by the Federal Reserve Bank of Minneapolis and economist Edward N. Wolff of New York University reveal that 35 per cent of the national wealth is held by 1 percent of the population. Centralization not only has consequences for the average man's net worth, but for people's perception of their power. Under excessive centralization, with its techniques for propaganda, citizens become accustomed to the status quo and forget that things were ever done, or could be done, differently.

As we have heard many times, the Chinese character for "crisis" also means "opportunity." The present collapse of our economy is a blessing in disguise. E.F. Schumacher advised us years ago to rethink our ideas of scale and to ponder the idea that in the economic and social spheres "small is beautiful." I will add that only the relative smallness of a region will allow for the creation of a human-centered society, one that can nurture the individual to full development.

The establishment of decentralized regional economies and cultures is a prerequisite for the reestablishment of the human being at the center of society, not at the periphery, where we are at present. The following essays are intended to make the present state of affairs clear beyond question, and to offer hope in projects across the globe that have enhanced local and regional self-reliance and self-sufficiency. These projects include closed agricultural systems, manufacturing and farm cooperatives, the Grameen Bank of Bangladesh, the Bank of North Dakota, and more. These proven experiments could be harnessed to create thriving, self-reliant and self-sufficient regional economies that now seem beyond our dreams.

# PART ONE

# CHAPTER ONE

*WHOSE GAME DO WE PLAY? THEIRS OR OURS?*

Lewis Mumford, a writer and generalist and one of the last of our public intellectuals, coined the word "megamachine," which means "big machine." This and the phrase "Power Complex" were Mumford's words for America's industrial-military complex.

Like a giant machine our system is composed of interlocking subsystems, including transportation, banking and finance, education, government, housing and more. Each is and has been for some time in crisis.

The immediate cause of the crisis lies in centralization, the control of power and wealth in one, or in our case, relatively few centers of command. As Brook Adams pointed out in *The Law of Civilization and Decay*, centralization occurs late in the life of a civilization. In our case, it is complicated by a Byzantine bureaucracy.

The American economy is centralized by virtue of market concentration, which means that small clusters of corporations (oligopolies) dominate each market sector. Thus in 2014 four mega-banks—Wells-Fargo, JP Morgan Chase, Bank of America and Citigroup—dominated banking and finance, and still do. They are the largest of the "too-big-to-fail banks." With their financial meltdown the world's economic system was pushed to the brink.

In agriculture, concentration has meant that a handful of corporations control various facets of food production and distribution. Over 80 percent of seed production, for example, is controlled by Monsanto and DuPont. Another four corporations—Tyson, Cargill, JBS USA, and National Beef Packing—control over 80 percent of the beef packing market. The same situation occurs in all other areas of food production.

Media is controlled by a handful of global conglomerates. In 2012, GE, Rupert Murdoch's News Corporation, Disney, Viacom, Time-Warner, and CBS controlled 90 percent of the media in America. After GE sold NBC to Comcast in 2013, Comcast became the largest media conglomerate.

And so it goes in each sector of the economy, in which many of the giants have interlocking boards of directors.

So what is the problem with market concentration? Economists laud the efficiency and lower production costs gained through market concentration, which in turn enables giant corporations to pass lower retail prices to consumers. The problem is, the system is failing too many Americans. Corporate downsizing and outsourcing, along with mechanization, have left many without work. Others can only find part-time employment. The U.S. Census Bureau reported that in 2013, 45.3 million people lived below the federal poverty level.

Let us think of the megamachine with all of its subsystems as a kind of game that can be played only so long as enough players agree to the rules. If enough players opt out, the game collapses. Disgruntled players, finding that the rules are rigged in favor of the dealer, may decide to play a different game. For example, tired of not getting a fair shake from the game that agribusiness plays, the people of the sustainable agriculture movement have opted to play their own game.

If the people in a region have not devised their own economic game, they must play by the rules that the culture at large sets for them and remain subject to the whims of a game they cannot control.

*A sustainable, self-reliant economy developed on a grassroots level for the benefit of locals need not wait for the collapse of the present system.* Indeed, as American well being depends ultimately upon a financial system whose speculation is poorly regulated, the sooner we get a move on the better.

Only a region is large enough to play its own game with its own rules—successfully. Its birth will depend upon many smaller births, the creation of smaller games being played across a region. Each of the smaller games, such as local and regional energy production with wind turbines, solar fields and small hydroelectric plants is an adventure in self-reliance. Local barter enables players to obtain goods and services while strengthening social bonds. Micro-lending circles enable them to develop or expand their own small businesses. Community development banks investing within the region and not locked into the mega-banking system will provide capital for the creation of larger businesses.

As more games are played successfully, they attract more

players. The local foods systems movement is the best example of an alternative economic game that comes to mind. It is rapidly growing and will continue growing as more people become aware of the health risks created by industrial agriculture.

Several years ago a planning consultant submitted a report to my present city of residence, Decorah, Iowa. The report was titled, "Sustainable Decorah." "Sustainable Decorah" or "Sustainable Any City" is a concept that can only have meaning within a context embracing more than the confines of a city's limits. No city or town can sustain itself. Every city's health depends in large measure on the health of the cities that supply it with industrial goods and the farms that provide it with food. Just as no man is an island, so too no city is an island.

To be truly sustainable we must look across county and state lines to work on cooperative development with the producers of arts and commerce in our regions.

*Rural America must become more self-reliant and self-sufficient if it hopes to avoid the trauma of another national Depression. Then and now I believe that it is imperative that we in rural America build self-reliant regional economies, and that this can only be done on a grassroots level.*

Too many of our local, state, and national politicians, and our courts, function at the behest of Money. And while the building of a regional economy will at times have to call upon courts and public officials, the heavy lifting can only be done by us, the non-elected citizens. Ultimately we have only ourselves to rely on, and the sooner we get a move on, the better.

# CHAPTER TWO

*TOO BIG, TOO COMPLEX*

One of the distinguishing features of contemporary American civilization is the frequency of breakdowns and failures in industry, government, and society itself. The size of the problem is enormous.

When we look for other common causes of our breakdowns and their frequency, we begin to suspect that the sheer size and complexity of the American system is implicated. Each function of our economy, such as transportation, is a highly complex system with multiple subsystems.

Both the systems and their subsystems are the product of rigid methods. Engineering, for example, operates by formulae. Contemporary warfare relies on drone attack. Stock trading by mega-investors and institutions now relies on highly complex mathematical formulae.

Each subsystem has been created and is directed by specialists. These have been trained in rigid methods whose aim is to transform all activity into smoothly running machines, which yield predictable results. The specialists' rigid methods are the product of reason devoid of common sense or imagination. This is System.

System is what the bureaucrat, engineer, and industrialist want. It is what the elites governing our society want. System is created and directed by reason—reason, I repeat, unaided by common sense, imagination, or love; therefore it becomes inhuman. Yet it is supposed to solve any problem.

Rigidity is not equivalent to complexity. But the rigidity of System, combined with the size and complexity of its parts, insures instability. Those who design our bureaucracies and corporate departments share the same mind set, therefore what they produce is a product of that mind set. The non-specialist who is capable of looking at the world with what the specialist would call naïve eyes, intuitively understands that complexity such as ours is inherently unstable. The elite specialist, however, looks outside the system for causes of instability. After all, the system is a creation of reason, which cannot be faulted. We find confirmation of this blindness in a paper written by Joel Cutcher-Gershenfeld and Eric Rebentisch for an MIT engineering symposium. Their paper's title, "The Impact of Instability on Complex Technical and Social Systems," states that the source of instability comes from outside the system. Instability, they claim, "occurs when a system responds to external stimuli in a way that makes the system less controllable. . ."

But what is this other than to say that rational systems, since they are highly vulnerable to external stimuli, are inherently unstable?

I now offer well-known examples of breakdowns, failures and crises from finance, industry and government that should convince even the unbelieving that the size of these systems has grown too large and too complex. Moreover, I repeat, each system is the product of rigid method. The time has come to rebuild our culture to fit the human being and not to contort the human being to fit a desiccated, inhuman System.

The sheer size of our government agencies and corporations ensures that, salary aside, the individual manager or worker has no personal stake in whatever is produced or provided. And why should he? His name is not on the work produced. Whether the failures and breakdowns in the following are the result of size or complexity, or both, I leave the reader to decide.

*Infrastructure:* The American Society of Civil Engineers issues a report card on U.S. infrastructure every four years. The report covers sixteen categories—roads, bridges, dams, ports, aviation, inland waterways, drinking water, energy, solid waste, hazardous waste, levees, wastewater, transit, energy, public parks, and schools—and gives grades A through F to each. The United States' cumulative infrastructure's grade for 2013 was D+. The future health of this economy depends on the maintenance of our infrastructure.

Example 1: Transportation. In 2007 the eight-lane bridge on I-35 in Minneapolis collapsed, killing 13 people. The bridge, designed in 1964, was not built to carry the traffic it carried in 2007. Not one engineer, apparently, projected traffic flow far into the future.

Such a disaster would not have occurred in a small city.

Example 2: Drinking Water. In 2014, in a cost cutting measure, the office of Michigan Governor Rick Snyder directed that Flint, Michigan stop buying its water from Detroit and begin getting water from the Flint River. Detroit's water is treated with ortho-phosphate, a chemical that coats pipes and prevents the lead in Flint's pipes from leaching into the water. The Flint River water, however, contains high levels of chloride, eight times as much as Detroit's. Chloride is highly corrosive, and lead began leaching into Flint's drinking water. Local and state officials and the EPA were exceedingly slow to respond to the crisis in which at least 100 children suffered irreparable brain damage as a result of drinking lead contaminated water.

*Military.* Despite years of air and drone attacks in Pakistan, Afghanistan, Somalia, and Yemen, the U.S. has not defeated its declared Islamic enemy. In fact, its strikes have served as a recruiting tool. The Bureau for Investigative Journalism reported that since 2004, the CIA has conducted 422 drone strikes in Pakistan, which have killed between 2,500 and 4,000 people. Still we see no end to our bombing. Despite its two attacks on Iraq, the U.S. military failed to achieve political stability in the country. Brown University's Watson Institute for International and Public Affairs notes that figures from the Iraqi and U.S. led coalition report that approximately 165,000 Iraqi's died violently between 2003 and 2015.

*Agribusiness.* Periodic cases of salmonella and e-coli poisoning occur from foods produced in giant processing plants. The worst and most publicized case of commercial food poisoning was the e-coli infections caused by hamburger meat sold at Jack-in-the Box restaurants in Washington, Idaho, California, and Nevada. One hundred eighty-seven people were hospitalized and four died from the contamination. The infected meat came from one or more unidentified processing plants owned by Von Companies.

*Banking & Finance.*
In 1999, President Clinton signed the repeal of the Glass-Steagall

Act, which was part of the Banking Act of 1933. The Glass-Steagall Act's provisions prevented commercial banks from buying, selling, or underwriting non-government bonds for themselves or customers. But in the 1960s, the federal government began looking the other way as banks began ignoring the mandates. By 2007 Wall Street investment firms, which by then acted as commercial banks, were packaging and selling "toxic" mortgage packages. These caused a real estate bubble that burst and sent tens of thousands of people onto the streets. The banks, poisoned by their own greed, were saved by the federal government's massive cash infusions.

*Health Care.* In 2007, *The Washington Post* reported on scandalous conditions at the Walter Reed Medical Center. One of the hospital's buildings had wounded soldiers living with rats, cockroaches, and black mold, but no heat or water. The hospital administration knew of these problems in 1999 and in 2002 Major General Kiley, commander of Walter Reed, denied funding improvements. In 2014, thirty-four veterans died while waiting for care at the VA hospital in Phoenix, while another six died while waiting for care at other Phoenix facilities. Veterans across the country experienced delays at other VA hospitals. The Associated Press reported that a White House investigation declared that the Veteran's Administration had "significant and chronic system failures" and a "corrosive culture."

*Education.* The No Child Left Behind Act of 2001 set national standards for elementary and secondary schools. Tests for each grade were given annually with the expectation that scores for each grade would improve every year until standards were met and universal literacy was achieved. However, teachers found themselves teaching for tests and not for understanding, and were burdened with hours of paperwork. The Act is being reconsidered.

*Manufacturing.* Since 1966, 390 million vehicles have been recalled for life threatening defects. In 2009 and 2010 Toyota recalled 9 million models for gas pedal problems that caused eighty-nine deaths. Over twenty million Ford vehicles manufactured between 1976 and 1980 were recalled for transmission defects that caused ninety-eight deaths. A General Motors flawed ignition switch caused 100 deaths before GM recalled 800,000 vehicles in 2014. The complete list of recalls and deaths is far longer.

*Federal Government: Legislative Branch.* Little need be said about our dysfunctional Congress. Due to the rancor between Democrats and Republicans, no significant legislation has passed Congress in several years. A comparison of the speeches and writings of current senators and representatives with those of our country's founders shows the current crop's intellectual nullity. The fact that they refuse to enact a ban on automatic and semi-automatic rifles results in the periodic slaughter of innocents by psychopaths.

*Public Safety*: Police Murders. Repeated reports of municipal police murdering unarmed, innocent people have become a staple of national news. The attacks range from choking a New York homeless man to death to shooting a fleeing Chicago teen in the back sixteen times. The U.S. Border Patrol is another example of a police force that is staffed with criminals. Border Patrol agents are almost routinely arrested for a variety of crimes, including petty theft, drug smuggling, rape, bribery, and smuggling aliens. One hundred forty-four agents have been arrested between 2005 and 2013 on a variety of charges. A group of about a dozen agents were videotaped as they kicked and tasered and eventually killed a man hogtied under the bridge at Nogales.

*A system that is so big and so complex is inherently unstable.* Growing numbers of people recognize that a future even darker than the present awaits them in our failing system. If we do not have the will, the vision, or the competence to build decentralized, regional economies, we will have no choice but to endure a catastrophic collapse, which will cause suffering on a scale the likes of which we can only imagine.

# CHAPTER THREE

## *MECHANIZATION*

*"When men are merely submerged in a mass of impersonal human beings pushed around by automatic forces, they lose their true humanity, their integrity, their ability to love, their capacity for self-determination."*—Thomas Merton, *Thoughts in Solitude*

### *From the Organic World to a Mechanical World*

In centuries past, our ancestors lived in an organic world: Nature was alive, a living presence, a manifestation of divine energy: time was measured by the motion of the sun, moon, and planets, and the change of seasons: men then lived within the limits of Nature and did not yearn to become her "lords and masters."

For these ancestors the seen world was not the only world: there existed the transcendent— that which is eternal and unchanging. The world was a cosmos: it made sense.

Slowly, all changed. First, perhaps, time became Time, an entity unto itself. The tolling of monastery bells divided the day into parts; then came clocks, which broke those parts into hours, minutes and seconds. With that, Time accelerated.

Slowly, also, tools and instruments were devised to ease human labor; as the number of these tools and instruments increased exponentially, the curse of Adam was eventually lifted for many. The machine replaced the craftsman, and the craftsman and his skill and vocation were no longer needed. Other vocations were lost, and what the Buddhists call "right livelihood" slowly disappeared until only few remembered or practiced it.

As science twitched aside the last veil, the workings of the universe were suddenly revealed. Or if they weren't, they eventually would be. It was only a matter of time. The idea of a transcendent world was no longer needed to explain anything at all: all was matter or energy, or energy-matter. With that, the intellectual had effectively alienated himself and society from meaningful relation to the world. As far as Everyman was concerned, the world was no longer a cosmos. It was simply unintelligible. In the words of psychiatrist Viktor Frankl, man was searching for meaning; according to Carl Jung, he was searching for his soul. With such confusion, the easy answers of religious Fundamentalism grew rapidly, worldwide.

### The Sorcerer's Apprentice

Goethe's fable, "The Sorcerer's Apprentice," was a prescient warning on the uncritical use of technique at a time when mechanistic science had proven itself a powerful tool in harnessing nature for human ends. The fable is told in the form of a poem. A sorcerer has left his apprentice in charge of the workshop, and the apprentice, rather than manually haul water from a well, invokes a spell to animate a broom, give it arms, and have it haul the water for him. The broom does the work better than the apprentice imagined. In fact, it will not stop hauling water and floods the sorcerer's workshop. The apprentice does not know the spell to stop it, and in desperation grabs an ax and chops the broom in half, but now the two halves haul water. The water continues flooding the workshop until the master appears unexpectedly and breaks the spell.

Like the apprentice's brooms, our techniques—tools and instruments—keep multiplying. Some time ago this mélange of tools and instruments became more than a scattered collection of techniques—they amalgamated and became Technique—an automatic force—an automaton. This automaton includes any method devised to accomplish a predetermined end. Thanks to technique, commerce and finance developed into the entities that now envelope, permeate and determine every function of human activity.

Technique made contemporary centralization possible. Technique created mechanization, and mechanization created machine products—multiple uniform copies of a prototype. But it also created its social equivalent, the conformist society. Through the techniques of advertising and public relations, masses of individuals transformed themselves into machine products. The transformation continues, and as mechanical people continue growing in number, authenticity diminishes. But still individuals retain the illusion of freedom.

The mechanization of society is nearing completion through the ceaseless proliferation of techniques in every sphere and facet of life, from communications to the bioengineering of life forms, from advertising and public relations to nanotechnology. So ubiquitous is technique that each new instrument is blandly accepted. Now people line up passively in airports for x-ray and body searches. We accept that our e-mails and telephone conversations are monitored, and that video cameras are installed in virtually all public places. The tacit acceptance of the loss of privacy is a potent example of mechanical thinking. One of Mass Man's mantras is: "If you have nothing to conceal you have nothing to fear from (name the technology)." These are the words of a being that has lost the human dimension. What should elicit outrage evokes a few impotent cries. George Bernard Shaw wrote: "An American has no sense of privacy. He does not know what it means. There is no such thing in the country."

### The Mechanization of Life

As a teenager I experienced firsthand a highly mechanized society in New Canaan, Connecticut, where I spent many of my formative years. For four decades after leaving New Canaan, I traveled in search of authentic people, those who sized up the world for themselves, who refused to be molded by a culture created and sustained by advertising and public relations.

As I traveled back and forth across the country I noticed changes in every area of life. Towns and cities changed, of course, but more significantly, people changed. The continual influx of new techniques did much to bring this about, as did the growth of industry and government. On the one hand, with the proliferation of mechanical contrivances, daily life became increasingly mechanized. So accustomed are we to mechanical devices (we look forward to the latest advances) that we would find life unbearable without them.

In 1927 the German philosopher Richard Mueller-Freienfels took note of the proliferation of mechanical devices in American life and wrote: "In Europe it [technique] is a servant—at least in theory—but in America it is the almost undisputed despot of life . . . . The American sets an absolute positive value on technique." Technique was going to create another Eden. The home of the future would be fully automated; the housewife need only push a button to accomplish a task. Robots would do the rest. Energy would be powered by Our Friend, the Atom. Advertising told us that we would have "Better Living through Chemistry." When a problem caused by a particular technique surfaced, the standard reply to those who questioned the use of the technique was that technology would eventually find a solution to the problem it had created.

Even by the time Mueller-Freienfels wrote, technique was no longer a servant, it had become our master. In Lewis Mumford's phrase, we had become servo-mechanisms, not merely because some of us toiled at machines in factories, but because we lived (and still live) within a mechanical system from which few are willing or able to escape. Or even recognize for what it is.

Technique destroyed vocations and degraded the workman into a servo-mechanism. But technique has created a System powered by a hierarchy of Things—individuals rich and poor—whose only justification in the System's eyes is to perpetuate the giant machine.

The great study, which has only been partially undertaken, will be the explanation and description of how the human species moved from an organic world into a mechanical world with the concomitant disappearance of the human personality. That work will be an epic without a hero.

*So long as the servomechanism believes and acts as if there is no alternative to System it will not free itself and become fully human. Only by reclaiming the organic world within a decentralized economy and culture can we restore ourselves to full humanity. The Driftless region has the capacity to do this. It can recreate an organic world; in fact, it is in the process of doing so.* By developing renewable energy sources and slowly freeing itself from dependence on fossil fuels, by creating time banks and cooperatives and alternative schools, by creating local food systems, the Driftless region has begun the process of throwing off the shackles of mechanization and restoring itself to that organic world in which its original inhabitants and earliest settlers lived.

# CHAPTER FOUR

## *CENTRALIZATION*

*The Law of Civilization and Decay*
Why are so many systemic breakdowns in the United Sates occurring simultaneously? Why does incompetence seem endemic to contemporary civilization? One answer, as the second chapter argues, is that our System is too large and too complex. It is also highly centralized, which means that the powers of government, banking and commerce are gathered into great urban centers. In 1896 American historian Brooks Adams published *The Law of Civilization and Decay*, an analysis of the fall of highly centralized civilizations, including our own. In his day Adams was witnessing the rapid centralization of the United States, and in his historical research he produced convincing evidence that when past civilizations grew excessively centralized, they exhausted themselves. The result was collapse.

Contemporary Western civilization is very likely the most centralized in history. Consequently, centralization in this country, like technique, has become an automaton, an automatic force. Money and power, and therefore control, are held by a small minority. And despite its great destructive powers, the United States displays every sign of exhaustion. Its driving force is fragmentation; nothing coheres. Individualism, fear and greed are rampant. American society lacks any set of agreed moral or ethical principles, with large numbers of the population acting merely from expediency. The energy for effective, self-corrective action is absent. As Adams predicted, our country is about to plunge into barbarism.

But this condition was centuries in the making. Before Europe centralized it was a patchwork of localized feudal estates ruled by barons. In that period of civilization, the priest and the soldier dominated society, and imagination dominated thinking. As trade and commerce grew, merchants and traders grew in influence, and as they gained influence, pragmatic judgment supplanted imagination. Europe began centralizing to better control not only trade but the life in towns and cities. Society became less anchored in religious convictions, especially as the sciences multiplied. Now, in our time, with the banker and merchant fully in charge of civilization, science has become the handmaid of commerce and any self-respecting intellectual denies the existence of anything that cannot be seen, touched, tasted, or verified through instruments.

The consequence of all this is a narrowing of ideas and vision in all classes—in an inability to perceive possibilities. Thus this society has become unable to take self-corrective, protective measures.

Parallels between late Western civilization and Rome have been repeated often enough. Adams quotes the British historian Macaulay in order to draw one of his own. "The ruling class in Rome was a monied class; and it made and administered the laws with a view solely to its own interest . . . The great men held a large portion of the community in dependence by means of advances at enormous usury." The liberty and even the life of the debtor were in the hands of the creditors, the patrician moneylenders.

A person who borrowed money "could pledge himself, his family, and all that belonged to him." When the pledge was not fulfilled after a thirty days' grace period, the debtor was arrested and put in iron fetters and taken to the creditor's home. He could either be sold into slavery or executed. "A man so sentenced," Adams wrote, "involved his descendants, and therefore, rather than submit [to this consequence], the whole debtor class became *nexi* [bondsmen], toiling forever to fulfill contracts quite beyond their strength, and year by year sinking more hopelessly into debt" as the accumulating interest eventually grew to more than the original sum borrowed.

The greed of the patrician class and Rome's imperial conquests eventually destroyed the empire. So long as Rome remained a republic, her yeoman farmers were her backbone: they grew Rome's food and provided the legionnaires for her armies. But free trade brought Egyptian wheat grown by slaves into Italy, which undersold the wheat grown by Roman farmers, who were forced into insolvency and debt and lost their land to their creditors. As Adams wrote, "the cheap labor of those countries exterminated the husbandmen of Italy."

Our own situation mirrors this to a great degree. Like the Romans of the Imperial era, a small number of very wealthy Americans controls millions of American working poor who will never extricate themselves from debt. Since the perpetuation of the System relies on the heavy consumption of non-necessary items, advertising and public relations skillfully manipulate the public to insure continuous consumption. Credit card companies ensure their continued debt by charging usurious interest rates.

Further, globalization, spurred by free trade, has lowered the standard of living for millions. The foreign workers who have replaced American workers often work in sweatshops, sometimes as virtual slaves. This transfer of jobs, according to the Economic Policy Institute's Josh Bivens, has left the U.S. with a net loss of 3,000,000 manufacturing jobs between 2000 and 2005, the largest since the Hoover administration presided over the Great Depression. With no loyalty to their workers, corporate managers continue to reap profits while the blue-collar worker wonders about the future of his job.

In addition, Social Security's two trust funds, the Old-Age and Survivor's Trust Fund (OAS) and the Disability Insurance Trust Fund (DI), according to their trustees, may be depleted between 2033 and 2036. This, combined with the fact that only two percent of Americans have any savings, means that future generations of Americans will be unable to retire and will, in fact, live out the last decades of their lives in penury.

The absurd cost of college and university education is sending recent graduates into such debt that many are forced to live with their parents and possibly may never extricate themselves from debt. Furthermore, the credit card is a technique that, coupled with advertising and public relations, ensures the existence of a permanent underclass. How similar this is to the Roman fiscal system, which, Adams wrote ". . . coupled as it was with usury, was calculated to enslave all but the oligarchy who made the laws."

As centralization progresses, more and more land goes into fewer and fewer hands. Like the Roman yeoman, our small farmers have been forced off the land or out of farming. Technique and the centralization of capital created large machinery, enabling fewer people to farm more acres. Those small and medium sized farmers who wanted to stay competitive with big farmers purchased new combines and tractors and acquired a debt they could never repay and were forced to abandon their vocation.

In short, centralization eventually progresses until the few control the many: laws are passed and usurious interest rates are approved that lock the majority of the population into perpetual poverty.

# CHAPTER FIVE

*OLD INERTIA, NEW MOMENTUM*

Attracted by the beauty of the land, I moved to northeast Iowa with my wife in 1991. For months I did not see beneath the surface of life in the Driftless region and when I did, I realized that the farm crisis of the 1980s was not over. I began to think about how such a region could escape the trauma of another national depression, and realized that only a region that was self-reliant and relatively self-sufficient could do this.

The Driftless region is in the process of realizing that dream of greater self-sufficiency. It is attracting young organic farmers and gardeners, artists and entrepreneurs as well as comfortable retirees. The newcomers are energetic and concerned about global warming and the use of chemical poisons in industrial farming. They want to help create a more cooperative society. You will often hear them use the words "sustainable" and "sustainability," and their words are frequently matched by practice. My town, Decorah, for example, has more solar installations per capita than any other in Iowa.

Like others of my acquaintance, I believe that our difficult and troubling time will only become more difficult and troubling. But like many of my acquaintances, I believe that if any rural region can survive the future in relative prosperity, our Driftless region has as good a chance as any. It certainly has a better chance than most. After all, we could produce all the food we need for a healthy diet, and steps are underway to create alternative banking models. Public and community development banks, even microlending circles, are being considered. Many of us here believe that repairing the present system is out of the question. A new society embracing different values and utilizing techniques that work with nature—not in opposition—must be born.

This point of view is a minority view among Driftless residents, albeit a growing minority. If the vision of a self-reliant and self-sufficient region is ever to be realized, more of the majority must be convinced that our collective ways of living and doing must change. Cooperation must replace competition. Newcomers can and must be welcomed, not feared. Those who farm with chemicals need to understand that organic farming not only returns health to the soil but proves as profitable as industrial farming. And if renewable energy is to proliferate in the Driftless, global warming deniers need to see that the increase in horrific natural disasters have not been conjured up by the imagination of leftist scientists and media.

*Resistance*
When I first talked to people in the Driftless about the need to create a regional economy, I encountered disbelief. When I explained that a strong regional economy would lessen the trauma of another national depression, people thought I was proposing to isolate our region from the outside world. Some in northeast Iowa, with roots going back generations, were opposed to regionalism because, as a farmer friend told me, "They want to build a wall around northeast Iowa."

The word "regionalism" was unknown to them. It has taken decades for the idea to spread and for increasing numbers of people here and elsewhere to agree that regional economies are the only possible counter to centralization and globalism. If local economies cannot be developed and bonded together into a regional whole, what *will* deliver prosperity?

For some the very idea of trying to build a vibrant economy within the Driftless region was insane, literally crazy. My wife and I had a visitor to our farm house, someone from southern Iowa. He dismissed the idea. "It can't happen. It doesn't make sense." I came to understand that most people simply accepted that production and distribution of manufactured or processed goods would forever remain in the hands of giant entities. Still, I kept writing and talking about the idea.

In 1994 I wrote a six-part radio editorial for Iowa Public Radio on the need to develop self-reliant, regional rural economies. It won a national award, but not much attention beyond that. In this editorial series I was thinking primarily of the Driftless region. I thought that a common sense of place—a shared topography—would encourage Driftless residents to cooperate in creating a regional survey—a regional portrait—for the quad-state area.

I wanted to create a portrait that would serve as a preliminary planning document that would be distributed free of charge across the Driftless area. I wanted people, lots of people, to begin talking about cooperative economic development. This survey would enable planners to understand the region's assets and needs, its demographics and natural systems, all of which they had to know before planning could begin.

I remembered Chuck Owen, a designer I had met in Chicago in my days as a journalist. Owen was the design theorist at the Institute of Design, a partial reincarnation of the Bauhaus within the Illinois Institute of Technology. Owen taught his student a design methodology that he had developed, and with his students had won numerous international awards. I reasoned that if this methodology could create floating airports, houses, vacuum cleaners and dirigibles, that it could be harnessed to create a regional economy. In order for residents to embrace the plan, they had to be involved in deciding which businesses, industries and appropriate technologies were needed. Owen's method would be taught to everyday residents of the region, and under the supervision of Owen's graduate students, teams of residents would design the tools and instruments needed to create a self-reliant economy.

Two northeast Iowa banks paid Owen's plane fare from Chicago, and I recruited about forty people to attend his talk in Lansing, Iowa, where he explained his method. Anarchist hippies, bankers, retailers, and farmers from Iowa and Wisconsin listened to Owen present his method. The anarchists didn't like anyone making strong arguments for anything (such a person must be an authoritarian), the Decorah folks said they couldn't work with Lansing, and so on. I realized the futility of creating a survey for this quad-state area at that time. Bonding could only be achieved on a smaller scale, using sub-regional surveys of each portion of the states within the Driftless region, and then combining all into one.

*The Northeast Iowa Book*, funded by three Iowa colleges, was to be the first of the projected regional series, a tabloid with photographs, stories and statistics accompanied by a survey of this sub-region's assets and needs, all created by students and adults, a real grassroots effort. The survey of assets and needs was to be the basis for the design team's work. The idea for the book had not only the support of three college presidents, but of area bankers and most high school principals. The leaders of the project saw the need. Selling it to area residents was another matter. There was doubt and outright hostility.

By the time the book was completed, I was too drained to inform the public of its purpose, let alone of its existence. The president of Northeast Iowa Community College and I threw the 5,000 copies of the tabloid book into the back of a college van and dumped them off at strategic points. Since there was no publicity and no public information meetings, nothing came of it. Few knew its purpose.

Even while the book was in its earliest stage, some were violently opposed to it. The most violent opposition came the evening I met with a dozen leaders of one town—a newspaper publisher, the high school principal, and local retailers—who, after I explained the contents of the proposed book, found every possible reason for opposing it.

The local publisher became hostile. How was I going to distribute the book? he asked. You can't put it in a mailbox, he said, that's against federal law. Who is going to distribute them? Were we planning on simply dumping them in grocery stores? How did we think people would learn about the book?

He was energetically throwing up obstacles. Soon everyone else caught the spirit and they began arguing among themselves. I realized this group was not going to get involved and I was not going to waste more time explaining or justifying the project. I sat back and listened to them squabble for at least thirty or forty minutes before they decided to break up the meeting. During that time I said nothing. As we filed out of the room, an angry acquaintance of mine from another town (who was a friend to some of these people) whispered in my ear that this had been a complete waste of his time. Yet he had not bothered to try bringing the group back on track.

I was so exhausted by the effort of creating and trying to counter incomprehension and hostility that after the book was published I abandoned it. I saw then that the most fundamental issue to be addressed was the development of regional consciousness, that community development must precede economic development. Without a strong community of shared goals, growth is dictated by shortsighted policy, whether it springs from a developer's greed or the inadequate vision of town councils and county supervisors. *Only coordinated grassroots efforts on a local and regional level can possibly reverse rural decline.*

*Not a Technical Problem, a Social Problem*
Clearly, achieving greater self-sufficiency is not simply a technical problem. More than anything, it is a social problem. Many people here, as elsewhere in America, believe that our centralized system is a reality of nature, like the Atlantic Ocean or the Adirondacks. It is here to stay, or if not, it is beyond our capacity to alter.

A friend of mine, the mayor of a town in the Driftless region, wrote to me, "There are pockets of Northeast Iowa and the rest of the Driftless Region where people are quite insulated from the world of books and intelligent discussion. Too often their information comes from radio, TV, Internet and local and regional newspapers, plus social media plus bar talk and street gossip. Some people might describe it as ignorance, but I would give residents the benefit of the doubt and call it limited exposure to the real world. It might be due to a lack of education but it can be just a general knowledge gap. However, I have occasionally been a substitute for a local Trivia group that has teams competing against each other. These are some very sharp groups from all walks of life and most of them have many of your [the present writer's] concerns.

"Change is slow and you can't just change local culture and customs overnight. It takes a long time and sometimes it takes several generations—you have to be absent from the community for twenty to forty years and coming back you do see things have changed. Some have said, 'This town has really come into the twenty-first century.'"

Rural people, including not only farmers but small town residents, are conservative. They do not like change. An acquaintance of mine who served as director of the chamber of commerce for another northeast Iowa town, said she quit in frustration after two years. New ideas proposed by some chamber board members were quashed by those who said, "That was tried forty years ago and it didn't work then."

I asked another acquaintance in northeast Iowa why she thought her town was in decline. She had served on the boards of local community service agencies and said that northeast Iowa's needs were neglected by Des Moines. The money and attention, she said, went to cities and areas with greatest population, particularly the state capitol. That complaint is heard across rural Iowa. The upshot, said my acquaintance, is that people in northeast Iowa say, "You don't care about us; we don't care about you."

There are some notable examples of homegrown industries within the Driftless region that sell internationally. But they are the exception to a population that for the most part has lost the instinct for the self-reliance that characterized their forebears who settled the land. Western settlers, who could not rely on state or federal monies, created the institutions, stores, mills, and schools they needed. Today the irony is that many of the rural people who rail against the intrusive nature of government complain about how little attention it pays their towns and counties.

One line of hope, however, lies with the new arrivals to Driftless towns and cities. They offer hope, but residents whose roots go back generations regard them as outsiders, and often with hostility, since the newcomers frequently arrive with money and either purchase or build large homes. My friend the mayor wrote, "When we moved to town, long before becoming mayor, I was told you are either a part of the 'red neck tavern group' or the 'upper class elitists.' (They actually named the representative of both groups.) If there is a middle group and the one which is growing it is 'the Friendly Tourists' or FT's (f---ing tourists), or outsiders, as they're called by some of the locals. Many of the outsiders buy up river property and increase property values. As mayor I have the respect of both groups and capitalized on this to minimize the division between groups, and with the council work towards betterment of the community."

Whether they are liked or not, the newcomers or "outsiders" provide much needed energy and customer base for local business. So do those who grew up in the region but left for work and have returned to retire. Thanks to new arrivals, some downtowns are reviving. Cities within the Driftless would do well to collaborate on hiring a writer to market the region to artists and writers and young entrepreneurs. Artists and writers are attracted to affordable towns and neighborhoods. They revive them with renovations, galleries and theaters: the area becomes desirable and civic pride returns.

Rural towns with imagination should offer creative people perks to attract them. This brand of revitalization is a lot less expensive than handing tax abatements to a manufacturer who may decide to leave once the abatement ends.

Artists and writers aside, the trend of young families and retirees to move here is likely to accelerate as urban gun violence, economic uncertainty and fear of terrorism continue to propel people to seek a saner life. And why not here, amid a landscape that for beauty matches any in our country? In this lies hope for developing a thriving economy in the Driftless region.

# PART TWO

# CHAPTER ONE

## *REGIONALISM: AN IDEA WHOSE TIME HAS COME*

E. F. Schumacher gave us a great gift with his collection of essays, *Small is Beautiful: Economics as if People Mattered.* His book influenced many who pondered the interlocking questions of poverty, industrial production, and appropriate technology. Among other things, it proposed that the migration of people from rural areas to large cities could be slackened or halted by creating appropriately sized industry within rural regions.

He addressed the matter of rural development in his essay, "Social and Economic Problems Calling for the Development of Intermediate Technology." "A given political unit," he wrote, "is not necessarily of the right size for economic development to benefit those whose need is the greatest. In some cases it may be too small, but in the generality of cases today it is too large."

This addresses the crux of the rural problem; but it also takes on what is perhaps the greatest of urban problems—sheer overwhelming size. Schumacher was proposing economic decentralization by building business and industry in rural areas. In 1930s America, regionalists like Lewis Mumford and Benton McKaye were proposing the same remedy to address the imbalance between rural and urban.

The matter of size in government, industry and finance can be described in terms of centralization and decentralization. Centralization in America got into high gear in the late nineteenth century, and by 1900 regional economies and cultures were pretty much a thing of the past. As regional industries were displaced by their larger urban counterparts, the decentralized, regional economies faded and a homogenized culture replaced regional folkways.

Centralization and decentralization in themselves are neither good nor bad, and some degree of each is needed to maintain a healthy society. An adequate degree of centralization in a government coordinates the work of its bureaus and agencies. Centralization represents the tendency towards order and coherence; decentralization represents the complementary tendency towards individuality. Pushed to their extremes, centralization becomes totalitarian and decentralization devolves into anarchy.

*Mechanization and the Human Face*

The centralization of American government, finance, and industry has grown extreme, to the extent that it governs our life and work. Such a system cannot long endure, and our various environmental and social breakdowns are evidence of an ongoing crisis. There is an aura of automatism about all our activities, as though our technologies had a life of their own. Everything in our system is beyond the control of the individual. Our institutions and corporations have grown too large: everything exceeds human scale and has become inhuman. It is imperative that we construct political and economic units in which people can once again find a home.

Is there a means by which we can construct a society in which the human being is central, not peripheral, with an economy that serves us? One in which it is understood that Nature has tolerance limits, and that by crossing them too often we will destroy the foundation of our existence? Can we construct a society in which work is meaningful? One in which our voices are heard?

*What is Regionalism?*

Regionalism is precisely the means by which we can reconstruct society with a human face—if we have the collective will to do it. Regionalism is a form of decentralization, and is at odds with our overly centralized system, which seeks to impose uniformity in every sphere of activity. Our mechanized and centralized culture produces developments with cookie cutter houses, cities that look remarkably similar, and best selling books that are written by formula. People living responsibly within a region and whose sensibilities respond to the environment will create an architecture, art, and literature that is shaped by it. A poetry that reflects the pace, activities, and landscape of New England will necessarily differ from verse created in the Great Plains that seeks to interpret the life and environment of that region.

Likewise, a sustainable economy within each region will respond to the availability of its resources, rather than impose an agricultural or manufacturing system that has no place within it. Our resource depleting economy, for example, has been using the Great Plains as farm and cattle country, but to sustain crops and cattle there we have had to irrigate and are consequently draining the Ogallala Aquifer.

*Regionalism creates a home for us.* People find greater identification within an area demarcated by a common topography than with an area described by arbitrary state boundaries.

*Regionalism fosters local production over the importation of goods.* This means, for example, building with local materials, which in turn might mean constructing lumber mills or reforesting the landscape, building a brickworks, re-opening limestone quarries, and so on. It means developing a local food system. Money then recirculates within the region.

*Regionalism can work to retain its wealth in other ways.* It can do this by building community development banks to create local housing and businesses.

*Regionalism fosters a regional culture.* Regionalism promotes the arts as a means of maintaining regional consciousness. Regional consciousness in turn fosters a willingness to work together, which in turn creates wealth.

*Regionalism can enable rural America to maintain population.* The development of local businesses and the encouragement of entrepreneurs create jobs within the region, enabling the population to stabilize and grow. By creating jobs and otherwise keeping money circulating within itself, a rural region can retain many of its youth.

*Regionalism is what Lewis Mumford called a collective art.* The establishment of local food systems, local and regional industry, and cultural activities are all part of a great cooperative enterprise. The process of getting people to participate on a large scale will take time; but getting people on board, a few at a time, eventually creates a momentum that attracts greater numbers.

Early American history is replete with examples of local and regional self-reliance, from the Spanish Southwest to Yankee New England, from Chesapeake Bay to the Carolinas and Georgia. Indeed, if the Europeans who initially settled this country had lacked self-reliance, our history would have been remarkably brief. Who can say with certainty that the obstacles and constraints that Americans face today in creating a human-centered, regional democratic civilization are greater or less than those faced by our forebears who first arrived in the American wilderness?

But face the constraints we must. Today the lack of money

for local programs makes it imperative that cities and countries provide their own solutions to their own problems, with their own resources and funding. Regional projects, which involve the cooperation of several counties or cities, are far more cost effective than the same project replicated in multiple cities or counties. County school consolidation in rural America is one clear example of sub-regional cooperation.

*What Regionalism is Not*
*First: Regionalism is not an exercise in fence building.* Regional boundaries are indeterminate. There are no sharp demarcations between adjacent ecosystems. For example, the short grass prairie of the Midwest blends imperceptibly into the tall grass prairie of the Great Plains. And the Great Plains in turn blend into the semi-arid regions of the Southwest and these in turn by slow degrees are transformed into desert. An economy centered in any one region is bound to have close cultural and economic ties to towns and cities in adjacent regions, as they do today.

*Second: The regional societies that I think may evolve will not be governmental units.* They will not have legal status. They will consist of a network of contracts and agreements between privately owned businesses, corporations, and governments—federal, county and municipal. They will, of necessity, carry on trade nationally and internationally.

*Third: Regions as viable economic and cultural entities will not be the product of any government.* If regional civilizations reappear in this country, they will originate with and grow through grassroots efforts. Clearly no existing governmental structure, neither state nor federal, is going to abrogate its own authority. Local food or energy systems will be created by individuals working cooperatively.

*The Need for Community Development*
Despite their conservative tendencies, and because of the onslaughts of globalism, the argument for regionalism is now easier to make with rural Americans. For years have seen their young migrating to cities in search of jobs; they know how little money farmers receive for crops and livestock; they see their towns de-

populating and Main Street struggling to survive; they know that power and money reside in urban America.

As they see federal dollars for local projects disappearing, increasing numbers of rural Americans understand the necessity for towns and counties to bury old rivalries and work cooperatively for economic development. For we can only build a regional civilization upon cooperation and the recognition of mutual interdependence, otherwise we merely replicate our failed civilization. Community development is necessary for sustainable economic development and must precede it.

The problem of rivalries has not been solved, but a start is being made here and there. Individuals and organizations across America have initiated local energy and local food systems to increase local self-reliance. But self-reliance and greater regional self-sufficiency cannot be achieved simply by building a factory here or a processing plant there. If cooperation and the ability to look beyond short-term interests were not at root, the problem of economic justice would have been solved long ago. But the root of the problem is with us: our individualism has created our fragmented society. Enlightened self-interest must prevail. The alternative—individualism taken to its logical conclusion—is appalling.

# CHAPTER TWO
## *BUILDING THE AGRICULTURAL CITY*

*The Need for Social Bonds.*
For over 120 years rural peoples in this country have experienced the consequences of economic and cultural centralization. They have seen and continue to see their young migrating to cities in search of jobs. They know that the only large business in their town—the grain elevator, or feed lot, or mill, or coal or mining operation, or processing plant—is more than likely owned by corporations whose only interest in their town or region is in what can be extracted from it, whether crops, minerals, coal, or timber. They see their towns depopulating with empty storefronts on Main Street and remaining retailers struggling to survive. They see federal dollars for local projects disappearing. They know that power and money reside in urban America.

The ingrained American individualism that served in years past as a spur to accomplishment is the very flaw that is abetting stagnation and decay. So while rural peoples agree in principle on the need for cooperative undertakings between towns and counties, in practice they usually reject it. The situation is worsened within towns by classism and envy that create obstacles to community improvement projects.

*Rural America as a Third World*
In the early 1990s, after understanding the degree to which farmers and young people were leaving rural Iowa, I saw that I was living in the third world. But not only is rural Iowa a third world, so are the other areas and regions where people try to make their living from the land's resources. The point is easily made when we look at what third world countries do, then look at rural America. Typically a third world country has natural resources and human labor that it is willing to sell for a pittance, resources and labor that developed countries want, especially at bargain prices. As its resources are gobbled up, its workers and farmers become increasingly destitute.

And that description fits rural America, which exports its produce and livestock, minerals and timber, and in exchange receives a pittance. In the case of the small farmer, who was driven off the land decades ago, the profits from his produce, stock, and hard work went to someone else, usually out of state. On the other hand, the corporate farmer makes good money because he's farming in volume and receiving hefty government subsidies. But the corporate farmer, more than likely, does not live in rural America, but in some large metropolitan center like Chicago or Dallas. Thus the profits made from corporate farms flow from rural to urban America.

In third world countries, the industry and agricultural methods of developed countries—the colonizers—disrupt the traditional way of life in the colonies. It lures peasants from their land and villages for jobs in factories, mines, and deforestation crews. Likewise, rural Americans continue to leave the countryside in droves for opportunity elsewhere. Rural America's most valuable export, more important than its grain and livestock, its timber and minerals, is its high school and college graduates. They cannot afford to stay.

We see that happening, for example, across the Midwest. The present agricultural system with its high input costs of machinery, genetically engineered seed, fertilizers and low returns, having driven the small farmer from the land is in the process of eliminating all but the man who farms 4,000 to 5,000 acres. As I documented in *The Triumph of Technique*, business leaders have been plotting the demise of the small farmer for decades. His fate was written in the 1962 by the Committee on Economic Development, a group of economists from prominent universities along with leaders of large corporations that meets every other year to discuss one issue. In 1962 a subcommittee met to discuss agriculture and issued a report that claimed there were too many "resources" in agriculture, by which it meant farmers. The report outlined the steps that could be taken to move these excess resources off the land and into cities where they would fill needed factory jobs.

By destroying local and regional economies, the colonizers take away the native's self-sufficiency and replace it with dependence on the colonizers' economy. Once that is completed, control of their own lives is no longer in the hands of the locals.

That is the situation of every rural area in this nation where local and regional economies have been destroyed, first under the development of the national economy, later under pressure from an ever-growing international economy. In the 1880s, the Driftless region had a mixed economy of farming, fishing, industry, and commerce, all locally owned. Today the family farmer has disappeared along with the fishing industry, the lumber and gristmills, and the manufacturers. This story is repeated throughout rural America.

Meanwhile, no one in Washington is concerned about the state of the third world within its borders.

*Rural Americans Must Solve Their Own Problems*
From the urbanite's point of view there probably is no reason to keep rural America alive. The local foods movement notwithstanding, most urbanites don't know where their food comes from. Nor do they know where the raw material for their homes and furniture originates, and they don't much care. In the case of food, it makes no difference to most whether it is grown on a family farm or corporate farm. Big or small is irrelevant to the final product, which should be tasty, clean, and brightly colored, if not smartly packaged.

Clearly our politicians and bureaucrats share the general public's sentiment about our food, its source, and the state of rural economies.

I now think that Washington's indifference is a blessing. When President Reagan began dismantling federal programs, claiming that problems were better handled on state and local levels, I was angry. But now I realize that national programs cannot be flexible enough to adjust to local conditions. More important, a centrally directed program will not develop what needs to be developed: economic self-reliance and increased self-sufficiency.

We who live in rural America must realize that no one is going to solve our problems for us. We have only our own brains to rely on, and if they are stuffed with inadequate ideas we are going to pay a heavy price. No one from the outside is going to hand us a wonderful future. No one from New York or Los Angeles is going to hand us a three billion dollar check.

We create our own future. If we do not decide what we want,

and go after it, others will continue to decide it for us. *If we are actively going to create our future, instead of waiting passively for it to happen, we must first decide the kind of future we want. Which means we must work cooperatively: we must think together.*

## Capital Creation

So long as rural Americans believe that we can rebuild our economies and spirits within the existing economic system, our situation will worsen.

When most rural Americans think of improving their local economies, they usually think of attracting tourists or recruiting factories. We have all heard of desperate towns across America giving tax incentives and outright cash to companies that will locate within their borders. And time and again we have heard of these same companies, having gotten a free ride, pulling out for another desperate town or country where costs are even lower. Rural Americans would do better to create their own businesses and industries.

But this will not happen until rural America has banks committed to local development. Rural residents throughout the farm belt states can be heard complaining that the people who get loans are the ones who don't need them. That sort of conservatism is anathema to healthy commerce. Rural America needs banks like Chicago's ShoreBank, which for decades was committed to the economic development of Chicago's black South Shore district. ShoreBank rebuilt South Shore's prosperity by developing black businesses and making renovation loans to create affordable housing. Chapter seven in this section is devoted to a discussion of community development banks.

What does seem clear is that so long as rural areas remain third world countries, depending on the crumbs from the colonizer's economy for their maintenance, so long as the colonizers run the factories, farms, and banks, so long will rural America remain poor.

## Constructing Arks

I began thinking about rural economic development when I first heard Warren Rudman, in the early 1990s, claim that if the United States did not drastically reduce its national deficit that someday it would become the world's largest banana republic.

More likely, collapse will be triggered by another Wall Street bubble bursting in the not-too-distant future. Inasmuch as the U.S. Congress refused to rein in highly speculative financial instruments and Wall Street avarice following the 2008 collapse, there is every reason to believe that the next collapse will be even more catastrophic. This and other factors force rural Americans to think about constructing arks: self-reliant economic and social entities that can survive another national depression.

When I began thinking of rural self-reliance in the early 1990s, I knew that my nearest town, Lansing, could not possibly be self-sufficient. But what size area could be? For some reason, perhaps because of the shared landscape of hills and winding valleys and their farm economies, I began to think of northeast Iowa, southeast Minnesota, and southwest Wisconsin. I began to wonder to what degree this area could be self-sufficient.

Someone told me that this area has a name—the Driftless bioregion. That same person said the region included northwest Illinois.

I learned that people around the country were thinking of bioregions as determinants of future economic and cultural units, not in terms of the nation or of states. The important point when developing an ark is to think in terms of shared values and habits. A bioregion can provide this.

The Driftless bioregion unifies its residents by virtue of its topography, which in turn defines agricultural practice. Specifically, until the ethanol boom, farmers of the Driftless region built terraces and planted in contour strips to minimize erosion. But now, after some contour strip planting has been abandoned for the sake of greater corn yield, enough strips and terraces still remain to retain the landscape's character. But regardless of whether farm profits have increased, most of the counties of the Driftless bioregion are poor, about the poorest in their respective states. But, with the application of imagination and courage, this poor region could be transformed into a land of wealth.

In the decade and a half since the early 1990s, imaginative and energetic people from Minneapolis and St. Paul have been moving into southeast Minnesota; people from Madison and Chicago, even California and Colorado, have moved into southwest Wisconsin. And because of Wisconsin's higher land prices and taxes, increasing numbers of people from the Chicago area are crossing the Mississippi and settling in Iowa.

*The Agricultural City*
I have focused on the Driftless region because, having lived here twenty-five years and having conducted writing workshops for its farmers and village residents, I know its culture, its heritage, its history. It is here, confronted by the possibilities and limitations of the area, that I began thinking about regionalism.

The first thing that occurred to me was that a regional economy can provide an ark, a social and economic unit that can enable us to weather hard times. A self-reliant regional economy is not a third world economy, nor a region of the colonized.

A regional economy cannot be built directly, but in steps, and indirectly. In the case of the Driftless bioregion, the first step is to begin envisioning a Regional City for each of the four areas.

A Regional City is another name for what has been called the Social City. The Regional City, as it is usually envisioned, is an aggregate of cities, not of towns. The point of the Regional City is to maintain a greenbelt between individual cities to prevent the development of one mass megalopolis.

The Regional or Social City was Lewis Mumford's name for what English planner Ebenezer Howard called the Garden City. One of the chief characteristics of Howard's vision called for greenbelts between cities to be farmed to feed the local populace. Mumford's popularization of Howard's idea was chiefly responsible for the Garden City Movement of the last century. It remains an eminently sane vision: a melding of industry, commerce, and agriculture.

There are only three cities within the Driftless bioregion with populations of over 50,000 persons, so the Regional Cities Driftless residents might build are radically different from what is usually envisioned. But for both the traditional Regional City and that which could be built in the Driftless region, cooperation between population centers is imperative. If one town developed a technical college or a major hospital, ideally others within a fifty-mile radius would refrain from duplicating it. The pie, after all, is only so big.

Major economic and cultural domains, such as tourism, industry and transportation, would be addressed in common planning sessions to develop overall strategy.

In 1993 Joseph Lambke, then studio professor of architecture at the Illinois Institute of Technology, sent a proposal to ten or so small towns of northeast Iowa, stating that for $500 per town the students of his planning class would undertake the task of drawing up a blueprint for transforming northeast Iowa into a rural Regional City, which he called an Agricultural City. In my reading of Lambke's proposal, the land and the people's agricultural heritage are the glue that holds the region together. The price Lambke proposed was modest, and the insight that residents might have gained could have been enormous. But the towns turned the project down.

The importance of Lambke's proposal lay in the phrase "agricultural city," which unites two ideas that are normally considered in opposition: town and country. "Agricultural City" melded the two. To a planner, farmland would normally be considered negative space. But in my mind Lambke's emphasis on farmland imparted vibrancy to the region by seeing northeast Iowa as a whole.

This can be literally seen in certain parts in the region, on ridges, when you can look out over miles of rolling farmland. At these spots, the contrasting contour strips of corn and alfalfa, the woods, and the land dotted with white frame farmhouses and red barns resembled a huge and beautiful garden. And the development of that garden has been the actualization of a culture, not in words but in fact, a living process of man interacting with nature. It is whole, it is complete.

Thinking of land as focal point as Lambke did, it is easy to see how sprawl might be avoided and a network of villages reestablished. From a local resident of the Driftless region, I learned that area towns had generally been established eight miles from each other, the distance oxen could pull a wagon in one day. Driving throughout the region corroborated his claim: eight to ten miles outside a town I encountered either another town or the remains of one: perhaps a country church, or a church and abandoned country school, or a small cluster of homes. Smart planning, which is not necessarily consistent with a developer's plans for maximizing profit, would suggest that instead of expanding existing towns in northeast Iowa, that once these towns have begun to revive, these villages be reestablished. Perhaps these villages would be no more than a grouping of homes. Combined with zoning restrictions that preserve agricultural land, the region's rural character would be maintained while tightening the connection between the larger, established towns.

The remaining chapters describe the tools that could and should be built in each of the Agricultural Cities: a community development bank, numerous worker-owned cooperatives, and one or two closed-loop agricultural systems to provide fresh and vegetables year round. Each municipality would have a publicly owned utility powered by renewable sources. None of these tools presently exists in the Driftless region, but could be developed. *Collectively we have the money; we need the will.*

Needless to say, at present this scheme is utopian, for fragmentation wracks every level of society, from individuals to institutions to municipalities. The last large scale attempt farmers made at cooperative work came in the 1960s, but died when too few were able to put aside short term gain for long term cooperation that would have led to market control. Likewise, one of the biggest problems in small towns is their resistance to working cooperatively. At present, towns see each other as rivals, or potential rivals, and to complicate matters, most small towns are divided into factions.

Perhaps the situation will not improve, perhaps it will worsen. But the vision of a bioregional economy in the Driftless, connected by Agricultural Cities remains a possibility, and *a vision that is loved can be willed, and being willed, can be actualized.*

# CHAPTER THREE

*THE DESIGN PROCESS*

## Design

Building the Agricultural City, as I call the development of the regional economy in the Driftless area, is a design process. Design produces an object, but in this case the object is not a substantial thing like a chair, or house, or car, but an idea. The idea of an Agricultural City is that of a self-reliant rural economy and culture that strives to be as self-sufficient as it can possibly become, while remaining a faithful steward of the air, earth, and water.

The idea of an Agricultural City is not free-floating, unconnected to actualities; rather, it is grounded in existing practices, tools and instruments. The idea began with a vision, but the validity of the vision is demonstrated by the tools and instruments already used across the globe— in Spain, Germany, Bangladesh, the United Sates, and elsewhere. These tools and instruments, such as cooperative manufacturing enterprises, time banks, and closed loop agricultural systems, demonstrate that the monolithic, centralized system which presently governs the world, is not absolute: it is not the only possible world.

## Possibility

*I think of this book as an essay in possibility. The task for any region that undertakes to remake itself into a self-reliant entity independent of the centralized system is to examine the tools and instruments that can be used for this purpose, and to assemble them into a mutually supportive network.* Though no town or region can be completely self-sufficient, the goal should be to develop as much self-sufficiency as can be got. I repeat, the parts of such an economy and culture already exist, scattered around the world: the task is to weave them together into one.

## The Work of Collaborators

In order to promote the vision of a cooperative network of farms, businesses and industries, a network of collaborators will need to spread the idea of a self-reliant regional economy through radio and television interviews, newspaper opinion pieces, broadsides and films, a presence at local fairs and so forth.

A web site for the project will list collaborators with links to their web sites. Collaborators should be grouped by the service or goods they provide or produce. Organic farmers will be grouped together, so will machinists, so will furniture and cabinetmakers, and so on.

When collaborators within a group have a common need, they will necessarily begin talking among themselves about the need. Area furniture and cabinet makers might decide that they could sell more of their work if they had a cooperative showroom. Organic farmers might decide they need a gristmill.

*Funding Cooperatives*
This introduces the matter of funding. Since low-income areas often have problems obtaining loans from commercial banks for housing or business start-ups, the United States has seen the rise of sixty-six community development banks and subsequently the Community Development Bank Association. Sixteen of the sixty-six are association members, whose mandate is " to help the underserved," as the association's web site reads. A community development bank serving the entire Driftless region would help reverse economic stagnation and is discussed in chapter six of Part Two/

*Growth is Organic and Piecemeal, Not Planned*
The failure of contemporary civilization is due in part to its reliance on excessive organization in almost every sphere of activity. There should, therefore, be no more than a minimal organization to push forward the vision of the Agricultural City. In fact, a heavily formalized organization would be counter-productive, depressing creativity with bureaucracy. Nor should the process be driven by a master plan, but instead grow out of conversations between collaborators about shared needs. As architect and theorist Christopher Alexander argued in several books, particularly in *A New Theory of Urban Design*, a master plan is totalitarian: a strait jacket, if you will. A master plan is inflexible, and being inflexible, cannot take into consideration unforeseen developments. The design process Alexander and his colleagues proposed is one that

is piecemeal and proceeds organically, and applied to the Driftless region would be developed by residents, not by outside experts.

The piecemeal development of a regional culture and economy is not just a possibility. It is already at work in the Driftless region where there is considerable support for sustainable tools and practices. Renewable energy is already prevalent, and numerous organic farms focus on selling locally. New housing is often constructed with renewable materials and heated with solar and geothermal technologies, while a growing number of architects and contractors specialize in sustainable building.

As the number of collaborators grows through the web site, so will their recognition of one another. This becomes one basis for growth.

*Gathering Data*

Design today begins with research into local, national, and global trends: climate change, population growth, changing consumer preferences, terrorism, growing income disparity, dwindling levels of aquifers and more. Everything that will impinge on the quality of life is grist for the mill. Not only have regional and area surveys begun with such research, even furniture manufacturer Herman Miller relies upon it. More to our purpose, Italy's prosperous Amilia Romagna region with thousands of worker-owned cooperatives relies for its success in large part on its service centers, which provide the cooperatives with global trends information. The importance of global trends research should be the beginning of the design process.

*Constraints*

Charles Eames, one of the very great mid-twentieth century designers, said that "Good design depends upon constraints," by which I think he meant that good design not only considers constraints, but addresses them effectively. Put simply, a constraint is a condition affecting the design. In the case of chair design, the constraints include the nature of the materials to be used, the varied curvatures of the human back, and the environment for which it is designed—a home, office, airport, restaurant, and so on.

Consider one declining town in the Driftless and the constraints an economic developer faces in finding ways to counter decline. My wife and I have watched this town's storefronts empty out over twenty-five years. When we first visited this town in 1991, it had already lost many of its businesses during the farm crisis of the 1980s. Now, in 2016, about half the town's storefronts are empty. The blank windows stare out at you. The town is gray, without color.

No one has apparently thought of filling the empty display windows with art or photographs. The town exudes hopelessness.

Some of the constraints the town presents are its relative poverty, its citizens' spiritlessness, their resistance to new ideas, the absence of a nearby river or lake, empty storefronts, continual outmigration of the young, declining number of farmers, and absence of cultural venues, such as museums and art galleries.

Perhaps the most significant constraint is voiced by the city clerk and another resident. When asked what the city's biggest problem was, the clerk replied, "Lack of money." The other resident, quoted in a previous chapter, said the city does not receive significant funding from the Iowa legislature. "You don't need us," the resident says referring to Des Moines, "and we don't need you."

She expresses a hostility felt by others. But what is this other than a tacit admission that the city's residents lack the initiative and energy to build industries and businesses that could help restore the economy? And that they have failed to devise means to put farmland into the hands of young men and women who want a start in farming?

Yet another conversation I had with an established store owner in the same town showed that others are ready to explore and perhaps implement new ideas. "This town is dying," he told me. "We need new ideas."

# CHAPTER FOUR

*LET'S BUILD AN ARK: 1*

*"And GOD saw that the wickedness of man was great in the earth, and that every imagination of the thoughts of his heart was only evil continually.*

*"And it repented the LORD that he had made man on the earth, and it grieved him at his heart.*

*"And the LORD said, I will destroy man whom I have created from the face of the earth; both man, and beast, and the creeping thing, and the fowls of the air; for it repenteth me that I have made them. . .*

*"And the earth also was corrupt before God, and the earth was filled with violence. . .*

*'And God said unto Noah, The end of all flesh is come before me: for the earth is filled with violence through them, and, behold, I will destroy them with the earth.*

*"Make thee an ark of gopher wood, rooms thou shalt make in the ark . . ."*

Thus, symbolically, came one world age to an end. The same end is described in Greek mythology and retold by Ovid in his Metamorphoses. Zeus, the overlord of the gods, angered and disgusted by man's violence, destroys civilization in a great deluge in which one couple alone survives.

We, too, live in an age of great violence that threatens to destroy what is left of civilization. The ancient Sanskrit texts call our era the Kali Yuga: the Age of the demon Kali. It is a period of lawlessness, murder, lust, degeneration. No bonds once honored remain. Towns, families, cities are split apart with violence.

Humanity today needs to construct economic and cultural arks to provide for its safety and survival. A decentralized economy and culture that is self-reliant, producing its own energy through renewable sources, that can feed itself with the food it grows and manufacture the goods it needs, is an ark. At present, America is without even one ark, for each region is dependent on the global economy for its goods, and is susceptible to the global economy's fluctuations.

Ironically, "economy" derives from the Greek word oikonomia, which means "household management." But our global "economy" is no household and certainly not managed, but rather a chaotic maelstrom, including highly speculative finance that threatens to engulf everyone in one final cataclysm.

## Realization

If we in the Driftless intend to avoid the worst consequences of the impending global collapse, we need now to begin constructing our ark.

Everyone understands that a regional ark needs farms to supply its food. At present, we in the Driftless region, like the people in all other regions of our country, are net importers of food. The Driftless region is working to lessen the amount of food it imports, but this effort is centered around a few towns. Given the tools at our disposal, such as greenhouses and aquaponics, all food for a healthy diet could be grown year round within the Driftless region.

Now, agriculture aside, the Driftless economy is a service economy—a net importer of goods. But this, too, must be reversed, and can be reversed, by creating cooperatives for various sectors of the economy: a showroom for furniture and cabinet makers, a grist mill for organic farmers, a fix-it shop for handymen to rent tools and space to work. And so on.

A regional economy driven by cooperative enterprises would be a democratic economy. No longer should any region lure industries and businesses from outside the region with tax breaks and other incentives. Nor should local investment be limited to a relative handful of wealthy investors. If those with smaller savings and resources are without a mechanism that allows them to invest in local business and industry, then control of the Driftless economy will continue to remain in a few hands, and the condition of the greater portion of the population will continue to worsen as democracy withers.

A self-reliant regional economy can only approach self-sufficiency if it has created the means for local and regional energy production for home and commercial use. One local investor in large-scale renewable systems argues for the creation of publicly owned utilities powered by renewable sources.

Underlying all three issues is the matter of finance. Like rural peoples themselves, rural banks are conservative to the degree that a common saying in northeast Iowa is, "Those who don't need loans are the ones who get them." This is not true for all banks, but it is common enough to cause us to consider alternatives to small town commercial banks, namely public banks and community development

Now, agriculture aside, the Driftless economy is a service economy—a net importer of goods. But this, too, must be reversed, and can be reversed, by creating cooperatives for various sectors of the economy: a showroom for furniture and cabinet makers, a grist mill for organic farmers, a fix-it shop for handymen to rent tools and space to work. And so on.

A regional economy driven by cooperative enterprises would be a democratic economy. No longer should any region lure industries and businesses from outside the region with tax breaks and other incentives. Nor should local investment be limited to a relative handful of wealthy investors. If those with smaller savings and resources are without a mechanism that allows them to invest in local business and industry, then control of the Driftless economy will continue to remain in a few hands, and the condition of the greater portion of the population will continue to worsen as democracy withers.

A self-reliant regional economy can only approach self-sufficiency if it has created the means for local and regional energy production for home and commercial use. One local investor in large-scale renewable systems argues for the creation of publicly owned utilities powered by renewable sources.

But no cooperative economy can be built, let alone gain sufficient support to begin transformation, until a strong regional consciousness is developed. This is the beginning of community. Once large numbers of people identify more with the Driftless than with their own states, and once they realize that individualism obstructs individual and family survival, there is hope that they will understand that their best interests are served by addressing common—general—needs. Community development must precede economic development.

Paul Hawkin and others have made clear that real economic

development increases social capital—that it strengthens social bonds—while creating material prosperity. That is worth rephrasing: economic development that raises everyone's standard of living strengthens social bonds.

However, merely installing sustainable technologies is not sufficient to create a sustainable culture. If, somehow, all Driftless cities and towns and everything that depended on electricity and gasoline for its motive power were miraculously transformed overnight and converted to renewable sources, and yet we failed to transform ourselves, we would once again self-destruct. Unless we change, unless there is inner transformation that replaces competition with cooperation, aggression with benevolence, fear of our fellows with trust, we will merely replicate our failed civilization.

*Looking Backward*
People who live in the rural Midwest know that in the days when small farmers prospered, small towns thrived. The 1950s, recalled one farmer friend, was the golden age of farming. The small farmer made a good living then, and small town residents and farmers remember those years fondly. They remember that farm families came to town once a week on Saturday nights when farm wives sold their eggs for grocery money and their husbands visited barbershops or bars to socialize. In the summer some towns held band concerts on the town square, while others showed movies projected onto sheets hung from the sides of buildings and people watched from cars and chairs.

Today small towns struggle to survive. My own town, Decorah, prospers because it has a college that brings numerous graduates back to raise a family, but the six nearest towns began a downward spiral half a century ago. Two of the more dispiriting are county seats. Another town hasn't one business, not even a bar; it is a collection of broken shacks and houses. Another of about 300 has a tavern and a bank whose windows were boarded up years ago. The three larger towns are even dispiriting for the fact that they once flourished. Now half the storefronts in all these towns are empty. No one has even bothered to fill them with art, or photographs. Sidewalks are cracked and broken; potholes pepper the streets. The towns look bleached, colorless; its citizens depressed and angry, or like the broken buildings, spiritless. Drugs are prevalent.

This is the condition of numerous small towns in the Driftless region. Where can renewal begin?

.

# CHAPTER FIVE

*LET'S BUILD AN ARK: 2*

*Tools to Create Regional Self-Sufficiency: The Agricultural Component*
One of the major obstacles to reviving small towns and providing locally grown food in the Driftless region is that most agricultural land is owned or rented by large farmers and corporations growing commodity crops. The fact that the land surrounding small towns is in so few hands is a major obstacle to reviving towns and cities in the Driftless region. The federal government rewards big farmers and corporations with generous subsidies, which make their operations profitable and raises land prices beyond the reach of young, aspiring farmers. The result is that the Driftless region, and every state, imports approximately eighty-five percent of their food.

To increase the locally grown food supply and revitalize small towns, we need a strategy by which young people who aspire to farm can gain long-term access to land surrounding these towns. Local food production is one of three necessary steps in the process of building an ark.

*Land Trusts*
Theoretically, land trusts seem to offer a means by which aspiring farmers could gain access to land. A land trust is a non-profit organization whose purpose is to acquire land within a specific region for the purpose of preserving it from unwanted development. A trust may acquire the land either through purchase or donation, or it may protect the land by arranging for a donation of an easement with the owner. With an easement, ownership of land is not transferred, but its use is specified, even when ownership is passed to heirs.

If a land trust did own agricultural land, it could lease it to young farmers, but land trusts have received few donations of Driftless farmland, and none has sufficient funds to purchase land.

An easement, on the other hand, seems a more likely possibility for getting aspiring farmers onto land, and recent tax incentives passed in 2015 by the Iowa legislature may inspire land owners to donate easements.

*Farmers Markets and Community Supported Agriculture*
Farmers Markets are the best-known component of the local foods movement, and while numerous towns across the Driftless host them, their share of the local food market is, unfortunately, relatively small. In larger towns they are lively places of business and forums for catching up with neighbors.

Community Supported Agriculture (CSA) farms make a strong connection between farmer and consumer, and are popular among people wanting not only fresh, locally grown food but also a connection with the land. With a CSA, the farmer sells shares in the season's produce, usually for somewhere between $300 and $500 a share. The amount received pays (or is expected to pay) the farmer's input costs for gasoline and seeds and whatever else is needed. In exchange, the consumer gets a box or bag of food each week for the duration of the growing season. Typically the farmer produces a variety of vegetables, and if the harvest is good, the shareholder eats well. If the harvest is poor, the shareholder must supplement his weekly share with store bought items. By accepting risk with the farmer, the shareholder is brought into closer contact with the realities of farming and the natural world.

But CSAs supply an even smaller share of local foods than farmers markets, and do not seem to be the solution to greatly increasing locally sourced food.

*Greenhouses, Aquaculture, and the New Alchemy Institute*
Greater possibilities for producing locally sourced food comes from experiments with closed loop agricultural systems, sometimes known as regenerative agriculture.

The New Alchemy Institute, founded by three biologists— John Todd, Nancy Jack Todd, and William McLarney—began conducting pioneering experiments in closed-loop agricultural systems in the late 1960s. Their goal, John Todd has written, was to reintegrate "society into a genuine partnership with nature." The three were reacting against a science that, Todd said, aided "the triumph of industrial culture over nature."

What this came down to was the design of systems they called "living machines," systems in which the waste from one part of the system became the nutrient for another. Through their nonprofit New Alchemy Institute, they created two living machines—bioshelters—the Cape Cod Ark and the Ark for Prince Edward Island, commissioned by the Canadian government. With both arks they set out to create "a miniature earth. To do that we had to simulate the dynamic processes of the earth."

The arks demonstrated that it was possible, through solar heating, to grow greenhouse vegetables in temperate climates. The arks raise fish and vegetables and are self-sustaining, closed-loop systems. The fish are raised in solar ponds, glass cylinders 5 feet high and 5 feet in diameter. The solar heated water keeps the greenhouse warm and obviates the need to heat the greenhouse with wood, oil, or gas.

John and Nancy Todd left the New Alchemy Institute in 1980 to create another non-profit, one that would develop new processes to remove toxins from municipal and industrial sites, but their work at the Cape Cod Ark is carried on by Earle Barnhart, an early institute member.

Barnhart and his wife now live in the Cape Cod Ark. Barnhart explains the system: "In the Ark, each day fresh water enters a connected series of solar fish ponds, passing through them and carrying away waste nutrients. The water gradually becomes warmer and richer as it goes from pond to pond, and finally flows into a large cement fishpond. This water is used to irrigate crops and other plants. Ultimately all water leaves the greenhouse either as water vapor in the air or as drainage water down through the soil under the plant beds."

To my knowledge, cities alone have expanded the new alchemists' designs, and following their lead, are building large-scale aquaponic systems that will grow food commercially for urban populations. The Plant in Chicago, the proposed Vertical Farm in Milwaukee, and The Food Chain in Lexington are the best-known examples of urban farming. The Plant, established in 2011 by John Edel, is housed in a 93, 500 square-foot, former meat packing plant and the Food Chain operates in a 90,000 square foot former bread factory. The Vertical Farm, when completed, will occupy a five-story building.

The Plant is the furthest along in development, but all three combine aquaculture (raising fish) with hydroponics (raising plants in water) into what is called aquaponics. The Plant houses sixteen tenants (all food businesses) in addition to its own production facility.

The Plant, like other closed-loop systems, will use all waste from one part of its system as nutrient for another. The Plant raises tilapia that are fed on algae, duckweed and insects but will eventually be fed on the spent grain from a brewery The Plant is building. From the fish tanks circulating water moves the fish waste through two filters. The first is a tank where solid waste settles to the bottom and is sucked out and used as fertilizer for The Plant's outdoor farm. The remaining water flows through another filter, which breaks the ammonia from the fish urine into nitrates and nitrites. As the water continues circulating, it flows into growing beds—where the plant roots absorb the nitrates—and from the beds to a pump reservoir and back to the fish tanks.

The Plant is also in the process of building an anaerobic digester, which will take food waste from Chicago restaurants, groceries and other sources, compost it and produce fertilizer (for the outdoor gardens) and biogas, which will be used to heat and cool The Plant.

As Edel has said in videos, no part of this process is new, and the plans for the entire system will eventually be available on-line for free download. The Plant offers not only a powerful model for year-round food production in urban and rural America, but a blueprint for regenerative food production, and beyond that a hypothetical model for a regenerative society.

All three urban farms—The Plant, Growing Power (which is building the Vertical Farm) and the Food Chain—have a heavy educational component, offering workshops on aquaponics and other topics in food production to urbanites, especially urban youth. The Plant's aquaponics workshop covers five weekly meetings, a testimony to the seriousness of its educational outreach.

All three urban farms host farmers markets. The Plant's web site notes that it is "the only farmers market in Chicago where you'll find small batch coffee, gourmet mushrooms, kombucha, naturally leavened bread and fresh greens being sold in the same space they're produced."

Once its production increases, The Plant intends to move beyond its farmers market to include wholesaling its produce and fish. The Food Chain will open a grocery store, and Growing Power, the parent of the Vertical Farm, operates a CSA that offers fresh vegetables to Milwaukee residents in winter.

All three offer powerful models for rural peoples.

*The Sloga Project*

My description of the Sloga Project is derived from notes an organic farmer and friend, Greg Welsh, took during an on-site visit over two decades ago. I find no references to the project on-line, and I cannot say that it is still operating. However, there is nothing inherently impracticable in its conception; indeed, it is eminently do-able.

It is also ambitious. The project maintains (or maintained) 1500 dairy cows, 1500 goats, many more chickens but far fewer sheep. The goats, chickens and sheep provide meat (the sheep also provide wool), although the sheep are used primarily to graze the project's orchards. The goats and cows provide milk and cheese, which is processed on site. The goat milk provides both yellow and white cheese for export to Switzerland, while some cow milk is processed into yogurt, which is sold on contract locally.

The animals are bedded on straw, and when the manure and straw are collected, earthworms are introduced. As the earthworms digest the manure, their excretions, called castings, help create humus. The humus is used to raise snails (ten tons annually), mushrooms (fifty tons annually), and rainbow trout (twenty-five tons annually). This is half the trout sold in Macedonia.

The project has planted 5,000 apple trees and 5,000 plum trees—three varieties of each. The fruit is grown not just for human consumption but for the 1,500 bee colonies, which provide honey. The bees are raised on ten acres, which are filled with wild flowers. The trees are composted with the same humus that is used for the snails, mushrooms, and trout. The honey and fruit are both sold. In addition, the project has 500 chestnut, 500 black walnut, and 500 black cherry trees, which are grown to provide different flowering spots for the bees.

## Chinese Experiments

Under the former Communist system, the Chinese had numerous closed, organic agricultural systems. For example, the eighty-nine-family commune in the Pearl River delta produced its own meat, fish, and fruit, and from the animal and plant wastes it produced methane, which in turn was used to generate two-fifths of the electricity used by the commune. This was no mean feat considering that these eighty-nine families amounted to 90,000 people. Further yet, it sold its excess food to neighboring towns.

The commune grew bananas and sugar cane, and used the banana leaves and sugar cane fiber for fish food and biogas stove fuel. Water hyacinths and Napier grass were broken down in bio-digesters and also used to produce gas. Pig and human manure were also used for fish food.

In their fishponds, the Chinese generally raised two species of carp and one of dace. Plant waste dumped in the pond fed the carp, while the dace ate the pond scum. Treated human waste was dumped into the pond as well, and the resultant sludge was used to fertilize crops.

## Possibilities

We know that large closed systems can work and will operate for less cost than the total of heir individual components. Add processing plants to this mix and you have a system that could feed a four county rural area of 90,000. Such systems are not only an imaginative possibility, but a scientific possibility too. With adaptation for local diet, far smaller closed systems could work almost anywhere.

# CHAPTER SIX

## *LET'S BUILD AN ARK—3*

*Tools to Create Regional Self-Sufficiency: Creating Capital —
Part One*
One of the greatest obstacles to economic development in rural
America is the lack of capital. For example, if a group of busi-
nessmen in a rural county wanted to develop a system along the
lines of The Sloga Project, they most likely would be unable to
obtain financing from local banks. The project would probably be
considered impracticable or redundant, since an ample food supply (albeit most of it non-local) already exists. The lesson I wish
to draw from the example of the Sloga Project is that what has
been built and developed in this country is but a fraction of what
has been designed and implemented elsewhere and could be built
here. What has been built and is being built is determined by those
who control the capital. If bankers and financiers are unimagina-
tive and timid, backing only past successes, they are not going to
offer venture capital to innovative projects. And the Sloga Project
represents a work of great imagination, of a kind that at present
seems inconceivable in America.

## *Megabank Meltdown*
In a December 2014 article for "Economic Policy Review," a
publication of the Federal Reserve Bank of New York, Joseph H.
Sommer wrote : "Almost all financial firms are highly lever[ag]ed.
Debt-equity ratios of 1:1 are typical for ordinary firms: the wid-
get maker of the textbook. Financial firms' debt-equity ratios are
much higher: about 15:1 — 30:1 for banks and securities firms,
and somewhat less for insurers. This leverage has some implications."

It certainly does have implications.

But Sommer does not want us to worry. He offers us three reasons to remain calm. "First, financial firms maintain good credit
despite their high leverage."

Coming from someone inside the industry should we be sur-
prised   that Sommer offers industry's reassurance?.

Why, we ask Mr. Sommer, shouldn't we worry? Because, he replies, ". . . megabanks hold many assets other than simple debt. Some of these other assets are risky indeed. To reduce the variance of these assets, megabanks use diversification and hedging schemes."

Diversification? As in lots of increasingly complex derivatives traded globally from bank to bank?

"Second, high leverage is hard to measure."

Because bookkeeping doesn't apply. Collectively, the megabanks keep trillions of risky derivatives off the balance sheets.

"Third, leverage is hard to define, even if it is measurable."

Leverage is only hard to measure and hard to define in a world of derivatives where nobody knows the worth of anything because derivatives are traded endlessly around the globe. Literally. So . . . leverage is hard to measure and hard to define. Are you reassured now? Through the fog of language I think I see bankers and regulators and even the folks at Moody's winking at one another.

When the meltdown comes—and how can such a highly speculative pyramid scheme possibly succeed?—the megabanks will be well protected. We the masses, believed the media when they told us we were protected by the Dodd-Frank Bill. That bill assures us that the government will not bail out the megabanks when the next meltdown comes. That is true. But megabank lobbyists added the bail-in clause.

What is a bail-in?

The February 17, 2016 issue of *The Wall Street Journal* printed an article which admitted that megabanks "flirt with failure." "To avoid publicly financed rescues for big banks that flirt with failure," the article reads, "regulators globally have drawn up rules that would dictate when and how bank investors would absorb losses. Some bondholders would be 'bailed in,' meaning banks would be helped by, for example, writing off those bonds."

By a global agreement among big banks, bank issued bonds would be converted to equity—bank stock—when a bank faces insolvency. Austrian and Italian banks have already implemented this provision. The Public Banking Institute reported that in November 2015, four small regional Italian banks instituted bail-ins, with the result that one pensioner, whose life savings of 100,000

Euros was confiscated and converted into worthless stock, hanged himself.

But the same scenario can happen here. Former hedge fund manager, Shah Gilan, wrote in the on-line magazine *Monday Morning*, "If you bank with one of the country's biggest banks . . . those debt bets [derivatives] have a superior legal standing to your deposits and get paid back before you get any of your cash."

*Disappearing Community Banks*
In November 2015, Ellen Brown, director of the Public Banking Institute reported "Today there are 1,524 fewer banks with assets under $1 billion than there were in June 2010, before the Dodd-Frank regulations were signed into law."

The reason? Dodd-Frank requires such extensive and complex reporting that banks must add employees just to deal with them. That, coupled with increased capital and loan requirements, has eliminated the profit margins of small banks.

In a July 22, 2015 speech, Texas Representative Jeb Hensarling, chairman of the House Financial Services Committee, said the disappearance of community banks was an intended consequence of Dodd-Frank. "The Dodd-Frank architecture, first of all," Hensarling said, "has made us less financially stable. Since the passage of Dodd-frank, the big banks are bigger and the small banks are fewer. But because Washington can control a handful of big established firms much easier than many small and zealous competitors, this is likely an intended consequence of the Act. Dodd-Frank concentrates greater assets in fewer institutions. It codifies into law 'Too Big to Fail' . . . . "

The result is that small banks sell out to larger banks, which typically do not offer the customer service of community banks. On the other hand, the new capitalization requirements, wrote Richard Morris and Monica Grijale for Herricks law firm, " . . . may provide well capitalized community and small banking institutions with a unique opportunity to consolidate or roll-up other banks." The potential problem here is that the same mentality that drives megabanks may begin driving community banks. What we need are financial tools that will help rebuild democracy.

*How We Can Protect Ourselves*

We need not remain captive to a system that does not serve our interests, but in fact works actively against them. In small communities we still have bartering and lending, two uncomplicated, very fundamental human activities. So long as trust remains within our small communities, bartering and lending will be useful and perhaps essential tools for survival.

What we need are co-existing systems for creating work, building affordable housing, and creating worker-owned cooperatives. Micro-lending circles, time banks, the LETS System, community development banks, public banks and small capital investment groups can serve these purposes: They are means to extricate ourselves from dependence on the System.

## THE SIMPLE SYSTEMS

*Micro-lending Circles*

Micro-lending circles, which make interest free loans to their members, are little known in mainstream America. For the most part they are practiced in the United States by immigrant groups from Mexico, Asia, the Caribbean, South America, the South Pacific Islands, and elsewhere.

Most micro-lending circles are small: eight to fifteen members is considered large. Participants usually know each other, and their organization is informal, without institutional affiliation. Groups are formed and dissolve depending on the members' needs.

Each month participants contribute a stipulated amount of money to a common pool, which is loaned to one member. Members are usually self-employed, and from a wide range of income levels. Most use the money to increase business inventory or make capital improvements to a business, but loans are sometimes used to pay for health care, weddings, and funerals. The circles are based on mutual trust, and have nearly a 100% repayment rate. The most publicized lending circles were created in rural Bangladesh among impoverished women for small business start-ups. These proved so successful that they led to the development of the Grameen Bank, discussed below.

## Time Banks

Participants in a time bank trade for work and services through a web site. The time bank treats all work of equal value: that is, one hour of carpentry is worth one hour of dental work which is worth one hour of baby sitting, and so on. Participants and their skills and services are registered on a website which has an administrator. If someone in the time bank needs a baby sitter for two hours, someone may volunteer. The volunteer now has two hours of credit on his balance sheet and is owed two hours by his time bank community. Since participants do not necessarily trade one on one, the person who babysat can look for service from one or more participants. Perhaps he needs one hour of carpentry and one hour of lawn mowing: he can get these from one or two people..

For time banks to work—for people to continue using them—positive balances must be brought down to zero. If someone maintains a positive balance, meaning he is owed work, and cannot get a service he needs, he will in all probability quit. For the time bank to succeed, people must keep trading The person who had work performed for him, must perform work or service for others. Negative balances for service or work due must be brought to zero.

## LETSystem

LETSystem stands for Local Exchange Trading System. In contrast to local; currencies, like Ithaca Hours, which use scrip, LETSystem is a virtual currency. There are no paper notes; transactions are recorded by a registrar.

Here's how it works: Let us say two participants in the system agree on a job. One is a homeowner who needs a roof repair, the other is a roofer. Assuming the homeowner buys the shingles from a building supply company with U.S. currency, he negotiates a price with the roofer for laying them.

Suppose the negotiated price is $1000. Then, when the job is completed, the homeowner is indebted to the system for $1000 and the roofer is credited with $1000. This obligates the homeowner to enter into one or more transactions in which he will perform services or buy goods that will clear his balance to zero. In the meantime, the roofer will eventually want to enter into other transactions to acquire enough goods or services to "spend" his $1000 credit.

Like the systems that use scrip, LETS is a complement, not an alternative, to the national currency.

According to its promoters, it has three underlying considerations.

"First, it fosters community well-being. No one can claim ownership of it.

"Second, it is personal. It is created by the promises of the participants. The consent of the individual is required. No third party has control over the money and it cannot leave the system.

"Third, it is practical. It adopts the standard of the national economy."

Interest. The LETSystem does not charge interest. No one pays interest for borrowing money and no one is paid interest for keeping money idle.

Cost of Service. Administrators must be paid to assure a professional approach. They are paid in national currency. There are no volunteers.

Consent. Consent is required at all times. There is no obligation to trade.

Disclosure. Each participant must be able to "know the balance and the total trading of another account. . . . The balance shows the commitment of an account holder and the total trading volume demonstrates the degree of participation."

*Scrip*

Scrip or local paper currencies in the United States flourished in the Colonial Era, then disappeared with the First National Bank in 1791. They reappeared for the decade of the Great Depression but disappeared once again with the economic recovery. In 1991, Paul Glover created Ithaca Hours, a local scrip in Ithaca, New York. This spurred the development of other local currencies, including Berkshire Dollars, initiated by the E.F. Schumacher Center of Great Barrington, Massachusetts, now The Schumacher Center for New Economics.

Scrip and virtual currencies such as Time Banks and the LETSystem, encourage local shopping while keeping local dollars within the community. Virtual currencies have the additional benefit of doing away with the need for commercial banking credit and allow someone who otherwise might live off the fringes of the economy, unable to pay for services or goods, to trade for them. But there are shortcomings.

In *Sacred Economics*, Charles Eisenstein notes that local currencies flourish so long as their founders do not burn out. Once they are no longer involved and the novelty wears off, people stop using them. Sociologist Ed Collum studied local currencies, and in his paper, "Community currency in the United States," concluded that between 1991 and 2004 " . . . eighty-two community currency systems using printed money were attempted in the United States." By May 2004, only 20.7% were still operating.

Another reason is very likely the fact that merchants who accept scrip have limited use for it. The major drawback for retailers is the fact that since their suppliers are most often outside their region, they cannot pay for wholesale goods with scrip.

The global economy, as we know, destroyed regional economies. Rebuilding regional economies means building the light industry and distribution centers that will replace our import economy. Once those are in place and a self reliant and largely self-sufficient economy has been created, the solution for keeping money within the region is to create not a local but a regional scrip. That will keep regional money circulating within the region. The tools for financing light industry and distribution are discussed below.

The scarcity of dollars during the Great Depression gave rise to numerous local currencies, or scrips. Charles J. Zylstra, a resident of Hawarden, Iowa and a Iowa State Representative from Sioux County, developed a local currency known as Hawarden Scrip Money. Zyistra's plan and its success in 1932 generated such attention that the British Pathe News interviewed residents and merchants for a newsreel that further expanded world and national attention, with the result that Zyistra's method was copied elsewhere. In Chicago, newspaper publisher Winfield Caslow issued his own scrip, based on the Hawarden plan, called "Recovery Certificates."

The goal of Hawarden Scrip Money was to provide local employment that would provide workers the money to buy local goods. The city first issued three hundred pieces of Hawarden Scrip, each worth one dollar. Local unemployed were hired by the city for a variety of manual jobs, including street cleaning, for one piece of scrip and sixty cents a day.

Mary Trousdale Johnson, who coauthored a history of Hawarden wrote, "Each piece of Scrip Money was worth $1.00. On the back of each piece were spots for thirty-six three-cent stamps. Every time the money exchanged hands, as well as at the end of each week, a three-cent stamp [purchased from the city] had to be placed on the back of each one dollar certificate. Merchants purchased these stamps . . . and when all thirty-six stamps were affixed to the back of the Scrip, it could be redeemed at the City for one dollar. The thirty-six three cent stamps equaled $1.08, which paid for the Scrip issued, and an additional eight cents to pay for printing and advertising. The money paid to the City for the purchase of the three-cent stamps went into an account to redeem the Scrip. Thus funding the program."

When a Hawarden scrip had thirty-six stamps on the reverse side, it had circulated thirty-six times, paying out an equivalent of thirty-six dollars. When all 300 pieces of scrip had circulated thirty-six times, $10,800 in wages and purchases had been made.

A second issue of Hawarden Scrip Money was never redeemed: so many visitors came to the city just for the experience of using scrip that they left town with the scrip. The notoriety of Hawarden Scrip was its own undoing. Author Johnson noted that Zyistra was able to push a bill through the Iowa legislature that allowed each Iowa county to issue its own scrip. If that statute is still on the books, it could be of use today.

Local currencies regained popularity in the recession of the 1990s, but individuals participating in local currencies ceased using scrips when the economy recovered and the novelty wore off. Now, with widespread fear of a dark future for the U.S. economy, many towns and cities are considering creating local currencies. And those currencies that flourished decades ago but languished for a time are reviving.

Local currencies regained popularity in the early 1990s, but individuals participating in local currencies ceased using scrips when the economy recovered and the novelty wore off. Now, with widespread fear of a dark future for the U.S. economy, many towns and cities are considering creating local currencies.

In the United States the movement was popularized in Ithaca, New York and is slowly gaining momentum. Paul Glover, the designer of that currency, Ithaca Hours, writes: "We call our local currency Ithaca "HOURS" because this encourages us to think about the value of everyone's time. The name reminds us that the real source of money's value is created by people -- their time, skills, and energy." In Ithaca Hours, one hour of work is valued at $10. One Hour is $10; one-half Hour is $5, a quarter-Hour is $2,50, an eighth-Hour is $1.25.

Glover notes that in order to work, a local currency must:

"1) stay within the community it serves

2) be issued by the people who use it

3) exist in sufficient supply to meet the needs of that community."

According to the Ithaca Hours Home Page, 1500 local businesses accept the local currency. Since 1991, when the project began, $105,000 of Ithaca Hours have been printed. When someone joins the local currency network, they are given one Ithaca Hour; a business that joins is given two. In this way the amount of currency in circulation is increased.

The Ithaca Hours Home Page states: "Ithaca HOURS can be used within a 20 mile radius of downtown Ithaca (a bit beyond the borders of Tompkins County). This regional boundary helps keep wealth recirculating within our community." As Glover notes, when money leaves the community, people behave in ways that damage the environment and the well being of the community. But when people use a local currency they "Strengthen our commitment to the people who live here. Add to [their] local spending power. Reduce the need to transport goods and for excess packaging. Create jobs for [themselves and their] neighbors. Help set a standard for a living wage."

Paul Glover offers us an important insight, namely that " . . . we are often idle when all we lack is the means of exch ange. There may be plenty of materials, equipment, skills, time, goods and needs to be met, but we cannot work or trade with each other because there are no tickets around, no scores on the sheet, no means of measuring relative values."

## CHAPTER SEVEN
*LET'S BUILD N ARK: 4*

*Tools to Create Regional Self-Sufficiency: Creating Capital — Part Two*

*Community Development Banks*
There is a growing interest in the United States in community development banks, whose mission is to provide financing for business and housing for those whom commercial banks often consider credit risks. The Community Development Bank Association's website says, "Community development banks are community banks committed to helping the underserved." The association lists sixty-six member banks, only thirteen of which are officially certified by the Community Development Financial Institutions Fund, an office within the U.S. Department of the Treasury.

The first community development bank in the United States was the South Shore Bank of Chicago, later called ShoreBank. ShoreBank was founded in 1973 by four friends ". . . whose combined backgrounds," ShoreBank's now defunct website noted, "encompassed banking, social service and community activism. . ." They believed that a commercial bank, flanked by complementary development organizations, could effectively restore neighborhood economies." The four associates bought the declining South Shore National Bank with "$800,000 in capital and a $2.4 million loan from the American National Bank . . ."

The new bank's objective was to create economic vitality in the South Shore area, which was losing businesses and investment as white residents moved out and blacks moved in. The partners began seeking depositors by "visiting customers in their homes, sharing dessert in their parlors, and talking with their neighbors."

ShoreBank's investors included nonprofits, churches, banks, insurance companies, community organizations, and individuals. In an article for "The Stanford Social Innovation Review," one of ShoreBank's founders, Ronald Grzywinski, noted in an interview that the bank's investors understood "that the primary purpose 'of their investment is to do development and not maximize return on capital.'"

The bank grew slowly, but by 1975 it was turning a profit. Its website noted that "Thirty years later, ShoreBank has successfully lent over $600 million to more than 13,000 businesses and individuals in its largest communities. . ." In the next seven years, by 2010, ShoreBank had invested $4.1 billion in Chicago, Detroit, Cleveland and elsewhere, and had financed 59,000 affordable housing units. By 2008, ShoreBank had assets of over $2.4 billion and $4.2 million in net income.

From its inception, ShoreBank invested in minority-owned businesses and financed apartment renovation that created affordable housing. Its renovation loans worked in large part because the bank demanded that landlords live in their apartments for at least a year.

Although it took risks that commercial banks often shirk, its repayment rate was well within industry standards. ShoreBank's success was such that it established affiliates in Detroit, Cleveland, Washington, and Michigan's Upper Peninsula, plus affiliate companies in thirty countries. In 1986, Arkansas Governor Bill Clinton invited Shorebank to establish a community development bank and affiliated institutions in Arkansas, modeled after ShoreBank Corporation, the holding company for affiliated for-profit and nonprofit organizations designed to achieve the corporation's objectives.

Shorebank's work in Arkansas resulted in Southern Development Bancorporation, a bank holding company, which included Elk Horn Bank and Trust, Arkansas Enterprise Group, and Opportunity Lands Corporation (for real estate development). The Arkansas Enterprise Group had four components: one for small business investment, one to provide loans to the self-employed, one to make business bridge and start-up loans, and the fourth to provide borrowers with needed technical assistance. Now named Southern Bancorp, the corporation has been a source of rural Arkansas revitalization, and operates seven banks.

Ironically, while Southern Bancorp survived the Great Recession, ShoreBank did not. When the 2008 crash arrived, ShoreBank's managers felt it imperative to lend to those most affected by the crash. As a result, ShoreBank had $42 million in loan losses by the end of 2008. In 2009, Shorebank applied for an injection of $200 million from investors and the U.S. Treasury. While the money received from private investors exceeded the bank' request, it was to be held in escrow until Treasury came forward with the requested $73 million. Treasury refused a bailout.

In August 2010, the *Chicago Tribune* reported that Shorebank's assets had been acquired by Urban Partnership, a group of twelve large institutions, including Bank of America, JP Morgan Chase, Morgan Stanley, Wells Fargo, and Goldman Sachs, among others. Urban Partnership continues ShoreBank's mission and is a member of the Community Development Bank Association.

Depositors were, of course, reimbursed by the FDIC up to the $250,000 limit. Sheila Bair, then FDIC chair, argued for ShoreBank's bailout and was even backed by Wall Street bankers, most notably by Goldman Sach's Chairman and CEO, Lloyd Bankfein, who called potential investors on Shorebank's behalf. But political opposition from the Far Right killed a Treasury bailout. For one, President Obama, a Chicago native, was friendly with Shorebank, which was an immediate cause for some (who had no use for a community development bank) to oppose the bailout; for another, Bair had been at loggerheads with Treasury Secretary, Timothy Geitner, before the 2008 crisis. These and other factors played into ShoreBank's closure.

## The Grameen Bank

The Grameen Bank in Bangladesh was once thought to be the biggest economic development success story of our time. The bank grew out of a system of micro-loans for rural women established in 1976 by Professor Muhammad Yunus and others in an attempt to alleviate the country's rural poverty. By the bank's own estimation, it had eliminated rural poverty by 1983, but today that claim is in doubt.

When Yunus decided to create his lending system, he contacted ShoreBank for logistical support and lending capital. Two of ShoreBank's founders, Ronald Grzywinski and Mary Houghton, with a grant from the Ford Foundation, helped Yunus with the bank's incorporation.

According to conventional banking, one does not make loans to people without collateral. Therefore the current banking system will never be of any use to the poor who want to work their way out of poverty. In our current system the poor have no access to capital and therefore have no way to develop businesses.

The Grameen system established voluntary groups of five to eight people, who, as the bank's previous website said, provided "mutual, morally binding group guarantees in lieu of collateral required by conventional banks." Participants and their projects were selected carefully. Two people were selected for the first loans; if they repaid them, two more members were selected, and so on. According to the former website, the fact that these small loans were repaid in fifty installments, that participants and project were selected rigorously, and that peer pressure was applied on circle members, all contributed to the system's 97 percent repayment rate.

The website stated : "The assumption is that if individual borrowers are given access to credit, they will be able to identify and engage in viable income-generating activities—simple processing such as lime-making, manufacturing such as pottery, weaving, and garment sewing, storage and marketing and transport services . . . "

Expanding beyond its circle loans, the bank began financing businesses that built on those established by its circle borrowers, beginning with fisheries and irrigation projects. But, the previous website stated, these ventures grew to such an extent that the bank created independent organizations: "The fisheries project became the Grameen Fisheries Foundation. The irrigation project became the Grameen Krishi Foundation. The international replication and health programs were put under the Grameen Trust."

The bank later established the Grameen Mission Fund, whose objectives remain the same as the Grameen Bank, but provides venture capital finance, with an emphasis on innovative high tech projects. A few among the many companies financed by the fund are:

Grameen Cybernet Limited, which provides internet service;

Gonoshasthaya Grameen Textile MIlls Limited;

Grameen Software Limited;

National Soya Food Industry Ltd.

Grameen Shakti, a renewable energy company.

Because of the publicity that micro-credit projects, such as the Grameen Bank, were receiving in the 1980s, celebrities began touting micro-credit as a cure for third-world poverty. Banks and other for-profit institutions began setting up projects around the globe, and these, as best I can make out from conflicting articles, are what destroyed micro-credit's reputation. With the takeover of for-profit institutions, such as CitiBank, micro-credit became one part of micro-finance, which, in addition to loans, offered insurance and savings accounts, everything one would presumably need to transform a peasant into a western bourgeois.

Whereas the non-profits had been issuing loans at low

interest, the for-profit institutions levied interest rates that the poor could not possibly repay. According to the online journal, *The New Internationalist*, even the Grameen Bank began charging interest—at 20 percent. But that is low compared with other banks, which charge 70 percent. The global average is 37.

All of these interest rates are obscene: usury at its vilest, and at these rates the poor cannot possibly work their way out of poverty.

Another reason for the failure of micro-finance projects lay with the fact that borrowers were not trained and no market research was conducted to determine if the product was duplicating an already glutted market. The upshot was that too many borrowers made the same products or provided the same services. Only those micro-credit systems which provided training and market analysis succeeded.

Yet, in 2006 after the Grameen Bank's micro-credit program had failed to raise the standard of living for most rural Bangladesh, Yunus and the Grameen Bank shared the Nobel Peace Prize. Not long after that, negative reviews of micro-finance began appearing. Chief among critics was Milford Bateman, who spent years as an economic development consultant in developing countries.

Bateman conflates micro-credit and micro-finance, thus loading his argument from the outset against micro-credit. His criticism is unsparing and one-sided: he avoids mentioning the two reasons for the failure of most micro-finance projects. First, he does not mention the usurious interest rates; second, he does not investigate why some micro-credit projects work. In an extended thread following his on-line article, "The Next Monday," he steadfastly refuses to judge whether those micro-credit projects, such as  India's Self-Employed Women's Association [SEWA], have succeeded because they offer support mechanisms, including entrepreneurial training and market analysis, which the for-profit projects do not.

SEVA is described on-line as a "union for self-employed women in India [that] has expanded to include 130 cooperatives, 181 rural producer groups, and numerous social security organizations within its structure."

The description continues: "Though SEWA began in urban areas, since the late 1980s it has been successfully spreading into rural India using innovative structures, such as crafts and producers' groups, self-help groups (SHGs), SEWA Village Resource Centres, and the Rural Distribution Network (RUDI) that processes, packages and markets the agricultural goods produced by SEWA's rural members. It has also created a number of technical and management schools in rural India, to upgrade the skills of its members, many of whom have never received formal education or training. Presently, 66 per cent of SEWA's membership is based in rural areas."

In other words, SEWA's structure includes some the same education and support mechanisms that Bancorp and the Emilia Romagna region's worker-owmed cooperatives (mentioned below in chapter eight) integrated into their systems. A successful alternative funding system for the underserved typically includes a micro-loan program.

*The Need for Public Banks*
In 2005, the City of Chicago needed a desperate infusion of cash. Mayor Richard Daley arranged to lease the Chicago Skyway—a portion of Interstate 94 crossing the Calumet River—to a joint venture between two foreign corporations. For $1.8 billion the corporations will collect Skyway tolls for 99 years.

Three years later, in 2008, Chicago needed another cash infusion. In three-days Mayor Daley rammed through a parking meter lease agreement with Chicago's city council. For $1 billion an investment group led by Morgan Stanley will collect parking fees for seventy-five years. An independent consultant later wrote that the city undersold the lease by $1 billion.

Because street repairs cause some streets to be blocked off, the Morgan Stanley group lost revenue and successfully sued Chicago for $62 million.

How are other cities doing?

In 2013, Crain's reported that the Citizens Budget Committee declared New York City's debt to be $110 billion, double the amount from 2002.

This February, a Federal court approved Stockton, California's bankruptcy plan.

In 2012, San Bernadino, another California city, filed for bankruptcy.

In 2013, Detroit filed chapter 13, in the largest municipal bankruptcy case in U.S. history.

And that is just a small list of cities in crisis.

***

Most of the public debt of large cities is owed either to individual banks or to banking syndicates. When a municipal bond offer is considered risky, or too large, banks will group together in a syndicate to share the payout or the risk. Chicago's bonds, which Moody's has rated junk, have now forced the city to borrow at close to 8 percent interest. When city services are continuously cut and, in Chicago's case, property taxes are not raised, how much longer can the shell game continue until a city, Chicago perhaps, resembles Detroit or Camden?

Consider what the difference would be for Chicago and other debt-ridden American cities—even the small cities of the Driftless region—if, instead of borrowing from banks or investment firms, the same cities had their own publicly owned banks. These banks would issue loans at moderate rates to the city, which would use them for public works projects, or social services, or any other project that would expand the city's economy. The interest would be returned to the bank for future investment in civic works, instead of into private hands. Whatever the amount Driftless cities pay out to banks, the cost of establishing a city or county bank would eventually be offset by the income from interest earned. The aim of any city should be self-reliance, not continued dependence. Furthermore, the perpetuation of a small class of investors depresses democracy. A community development bank with hundreds of small investors would democratize local investing and greatly increase the number of people advocating for a regional economy.

The malfeasance of the too-big-to-fail banks continues to generate public outrage, such as expressed by journalist and author Chris Hedges. In the on-line progressive journal, *Common Dreams*, Hedges wrote, "Speculators at megabanks or investment firms such as Goldman Sachs are not, in a strict sense, capitalists. They do not make money from the means of production."

The conclusion that numerous critics of the current banking system make is that we need to decentralize economic power by establishing state, city, and county public banks. The current interest in publicly owned banks was initiated by The Public Banking Institute, founded by lawyer and activist Ellen Brown, author of *The Web of Debt* and *The Public Bank Solution.*

In her talks, Brown frequently refers to the example of the State Bank of North Dakota, established in 1919 in response to Populist pressure to shore up North Dakota farmers. The bank's account of its history says, "Grain dealers outside the state suppressed grain prices; farm suppliers increased their prices; and interest rates on farm loans climbed." But commercial banks refused to buy the bank's bonds that would finance the bank's lending, consequently its proposed scope was narrowed and now the bank makes limited commercial loans, and these in conjunction with commercial banks.

North Dakota Bank president, Eric Hardmeyer, told Mother Jones that in addition to granting commercial and student loans, and acting as a clearing house for other North Dakota banks, "We also provide a dividend back to the state. Probably this year we'll make somewhere north of $60 million, and we will turn over about half of our profits back to the state general fund. And so over the last 10, 12 years, we've turned back a third of a billion dollars just to the general fund to offset taxes or to aid in funding public sector types of needs."

This is the great appeal that North Dakota Bank has for progressives. A group of Vermont legislators introduced a bill to create a state bank, but the Vermont Bankers Association lobbied against it, and instead of a bank, a compromise was reached. Ten percent of the state's revenue is set aside for state projects and commercial loans.

Seeing the opposition that Vermont and North Dakota faced, public banking advocates elsewhere are aiming for a more modest goal: the creation of city banks. Santa Fe, one of those cities, has a working group, We Are People Here! Founded by Craig Barnes. The group grew out of a series of lectures and discussions led by Barnes in 2011 titled, "Democracy at the Crossroads and the Evolution of Civilization." On his organization's website, Barnes wrote, "Initially, we actively supported the initiative of New Mexico State Representative, Brian Egolf, to establish a New Mexico State Bank, similar to the ninety-five-year-old, and very successful, Bank of North Dakota. These efforts were thwarted by the strong banking lobby. From this experience we understood that we could only be effective by starting at the county or municipal government level."

Santa Fe's mayor supports the locally popular idea, and the city recently conducted a study on the feasibility of a public bank.

The word is spreading, and initiatives are underway in major cities, including San Francisco, to establish city-owned banks that would  help retrench democracy.

# CHAPTER EIGHT

*LET'S BUILD AN ARK: 5*

*Tools to Create Regional Self-Sufficiency: Worker Owned Cooperatives*
The two final legs of our system are local energy production and worker-owned cooperatives. Without either one, the Driftless will remain dependent upon the global economy, which ensures wealth inequality, loss of democratic institutions, growing poverty and violence.

*Robert Owen and New Lanark*
The precursor to worker owned cooperatives were two experiments with rural industrial communities, the first in New Lanark, Scotland and the second in New Harmony, Indiana. The experiments were the work of Robert Owen, a Welsh social reformer and industrialist. By the time Owen began his co-operative experiment in New Lanark, he concluded that improving workers' living and working conditions—English conditions were appalling and conducive to drunkenness and abuse—would improve character and thus business.

Owen bought New Lanark, a textile mill and workers houses, and instituted reforms to better the lives of New Lanark's 2,500 inhabitants, many of whom had come from England's poor houses. In 1817 he instituted his idea of the eight-hour workday, established an infant school at New Lanark, and improved the quality of goods sold at his company store and sold them at little above wholesale cost. He was also an early supporter of universal suffrage.

Owen's success at New Lanark attracted foreign visitors, including heads of state, and was the impetus for other experiments that combined cooperative living and working. Owen's work and writings influenced Marx's collaborator, Frederick Engels. Perhaps the single greatest lesson Owen taught succeeding generations is that cooperatives can compete successfully in the marketplace.

*Rochdale*

The modern cooperative movement originates with Rochdale, a British industrial town. Having lost their livelihood through the mechanization of the weaving industry, a group of weavers met to decide how they could survive. In *Humanizing the Economy: Cooperatives in an Age of Capital*, John Restakis quotes one of their members, George Holyoake: "At the close of the year 1843 . . . . a few poor weavers out of employ and nearly out of food and quite out of heart with the social state, met together to discover what they could do to better their industrial condition."

How many Americans, conditioned to living under the federal poverty line, or marginally above it, have taken this same initiative?

Holyoake continues: "Manufacturers had capital, and shopkeepers had the advantage of stock; how could they [the weavers] succeed without either? Should they avail themselves of the poor law? that were dependence; of emigration? That seemed like deportation for the crime of having been poor. What should they do? They would commence the battle of life on their own account. They would . . . without experience, or knowledge, or funds, they would turn merchants and manufacturers."

The group of twenty-eight members, calling itself the Rochdale Society of Equitable Pioneers, collected two pence per week for four months from each member. When twenty-eight pounds had been collected, the society opened what was probably the first cooperative grocery. The store, guided by a set of founding principles, paid its members dividends. In these respects, the Rochdale Society created the model for European and American cooperatives.

*Desborough Cooperative Society*
Of the numerous examples of cooperatives that succeeded New Lanark and Rochdale, the most impressive is perhaps that of the Desborough Cooperative Society, which combined Owen's fusion of cooperative community and industry with Rochdale's example of a worker-owned cooperative. For us, Desborough's importance, like Rochdale's, lies in the initiative, energy and self-reliance its weavers displayed when displaced by the spinning jenny. Ultimately what they created was an extensive cooperative system that has only been surpassed in diversity of products in recent times. They, like the Rochdale weavers were forced to create their own livelihoods or choose between the workhouse or starvation. *Again, let us note how one hundred fifty years of mechanization in the United States appears to have destroyed the impulse to self-reliance and the imaginative capacity to collaborate in creating work.*

How different it was for the Desborough weavers who had to face the likes of the owner of the local manor who had posted signs on his boumdaruy walls reading, "Man traps and spring guns set here."

*Modern cooperatives: the Emilia Romagna Region*
We in the Driftless region, and elsewhere in America, can learn much from two European models of worker-owned cooperatives. One is the Mondragon Corporation in the Basque region of Spain and the other is the lesser-known model in the Emilia Romagna region in northern Italy.

The Mondragon Corporation began with a cooperative established in 1956 by a Catholic priest, Fr. José María Arizmendiarrieta, and was inspired by Catholic social teaching. The Emilia Romagna co-operatives developed during the nineteenth-century labor movement. Both compete globally.

The Emilia Romagna is one of twenty administrative districts in Italy with a population of 3.9 million. It has the third highest per capita income in Italy and is said by some to have the highest quality of life in Europe.. Its most noted products are among the world's great automobiles and include the Ferrari, Lamborghini, Maserati, and Ducati. The Emilia Romagna has an arts and crafts tradition, which contributes to the high quality of its products. It is also Italy's most productive agricultural region, with 700 farm cooperatives that created processing cooperatives. Altogether, the Emilia Romagna has approximately 8,100 cooperatives. Since Italy has privatized social services, social service cooperatives in Emilia Romagna administer these.

In an interview with *The Next System Project*, an on-line magazine, economic historian Vera Zamagni attributed the large number of cooperatives to its people's independence. This cooperative movement began in the 1860s and, according to Zamegni, "People were used to self-government and were not prepared to work for a boss."

Perhaps, as a result, one priority of the Emilia Romagna regional government has been the development of small business, especially cooperatives, which account for 30% of the region's gross domestic product. John Logue, an observer from Ohio's Kent State University visited the region to learn what he could bring back to strengthen Ohio's economy. In an on-line article, "Economics, Cooperation, and Employee Ownership: The Emilia Romagna model – in more detail," Logue noted that the region "has developed a high degree of social capital," demonstrating that its people trust each other and therefore collaborate.

Firms that manufacture the same product are connected by informal flexible networks and collaborate to fill orders. The firms are known to each other and held together by mutual trust. They are small family-owned companies or worker-owned cooperatives employing ten to twenty people. They are highly specialized and technologically sophisticated.

When one firm receives an order, it subcontracts parts of

it to others that specialize in some aspect of production. The firm that receives the contract may change. When a large international order arrives, small cooperatives will collaborate to fill it. This is why, for example, the Emilia Romagna's numerous small ceramics co-ops can sell their high-end ceramics to the wealthiest top 3 per cent of the Chinese population—a pool between 30 and 40 million people.

In "The Emilian Model—Profile of a Cooperative Economy," John Restakis writes, "At any step of the production process, the small scale of operations allows the individual firms to make adjustments to the product, to respond to new requirements from the client, or to seek additional expertise if it is required. Flexibility is built in. Moreover, most of these deals are made on a handshake. Legal contracts are unnecessary and rare, and the transaction costs extremely low."

The cooperatives have established other firms, including banks, insurance companies, and service centers to support themselves and their worker-owners. By a 1992 law, 3 per cent of all co-op profits must be deposited in development funds, which are invested in cooperative start-ups or in expanding existing ones.

The service centers are, to my mind, the most interesting of the support organizations. Restakis writes, "Service centers scan the globe for the most current information on markets, consumer trends, technological developments, and best practices which they then provide to their members. They are driven by the needs of the small firms they serve . . ."

The cooperative system has served the Emilia Romagna region well: its quality of life is considered one of the highest in Europe.

*The Mondragon Corporation*

In almost all respects, the Mondragon Corporation resembles the structure and working partnership between the cooperatives in the Emilia Romagna. Mondragon, the corporation's website states, "is a co-operative business organization integrated by autonomous and independent cooperatives that competes on international markets using democratic methods." In this it resembles the Italian model, as well as in the fact that the first level of cooperatives (manufacturing and farming) are supported by a second tier of cooperatives (banking, insurance, social services and education).

Mondragon divides itself into four areas of operation: finance (banking, social services, and insurance); industry; retail; and knowledge (vocational training centers, research and development, and Mondragon University).

One of the major distinctions between the co-ops of the Emilia Romagna and Mondragon is the formal organization that the Mondragon cooperatives have adopted. This organization consists in part of a general assembly and governing council, a monitoring commission (accounting oversight), and the management council. The Mondragon organization also includes what it calls "Mondragon Bodies," some of whose responsibilities include the coordination of co-op production.

As of 2014, Mondragon Corporation included 257 cooperatives employing 74,117 people. One hundred twenty-two of the cooperatives are located outside Spain, including plants in Mexico and the United States. The decision to compete globally with capitalist corporations has not gone well for Mondragon. Fagor, its largest cooperative with 5,600 employees and a debt of 1.1 billion Euros, due in part to poor financial management, filed for bankruptcy in 2013 and was bought by Cata, a Catalan company. But the corporation also had problems with two of its other large cooperatives, Caja Laboral—the corporation's credit union—and Eroski—its chain of European supermarkets. An aggressive corporation, Mondragon's credit union has twelve branches in Spain, while Eurosi has seventy-five hypermarkets and 475 smaller stores across Europe as Mondragon. Clearly aggressive, the

Mondragon Corporation is vying with large capitalist corporations.

*The Lessons for the Driftless*
If we in the Driftless are to establish successful, work-owned cooperatives, we must recall the ancient Greek adage, "Moderation is Best," and emulate the Emilia Romagna model by staying small and flexible. Content with their success, Emilia Romagna cooperatives have resisted the impulse to establish cooperatives outside Italy. That, of course, is not the American way of business, which is to seek unlimited growth. But continuous growth has led us to our impersonal, inhuman society and to the verge of collapse. Our goal must be the common welfare: anything less only perpetuates the despair and darkness in which we live.

# CHAPTER NINE
## *LET'S BUILD AN ARK: 6*

*Tools to Create Regional Self-Sufficiency:*
*Recycling & Renewables*

The subject of this chapter is well summed up in the title of Ian McHarg's classic, *Design with Nature.* Although McHarg's book is a cross-disciplinary work on ecological landscape design, at root its subject is at one with those treated here. For the subjects of this chapter—renewable energy and industrial and residential recycling—are ways of designing a culture that mimics natural processes. And in a world that threatens to collapse in the not-too-distant future, we will of necessity use sunlight, wind and water to heat and cool our homes and use scrap to repair buildings and tools.

*Samsø Island*

Samsø Island off the coast of Denmark has provided Driiftless advocates of renewable energy with the idea of locally owned, municipal utilities powered by renewable sources. An island of twenty-two villages and approximately 4,000 inhabitants, Samsø is energy independent, thanks to a combination of twenty-one turbines, twenty of which are locally owned.

With his own companies Decorah Solar and Oneota Solar, retired Decorah banker Larry Grimstad built arrays of 3,500 solar panels at Luther College for a cost of $2.8 million. The agreement between Grimstad and the college provides for the college to lease the arrays for seven years, after which time the college has the option to buy it. The solar fields provides about 5% of the colleges electricity and powers a student housing complex including its geothermal heating and air conditioning system. When Luther acquires another solar array, the two fields of panels will power the geothermal heating and cooling system at a cluster of student housing.

Grimstad describes how he and two other Decorah residents, Luther Craig Mosher, Jim Martin-Schramm, and Andy Johnson, "began having discussions over breakfasts and coffees about forming something to increase the awareness and take action locally. " The result was the creation of the Winneshiek Energy District.

The concept for the energy district was modeled on the nation-wide, county soil and water conservation districts that span the United States. Paul Johnson, one of the initial members of the breakfast group, was a former director of the Federal Soil Conservation Service, appointed by President Bill Clinton.

Based on his experience with the Soil Conservation Service, Johnson realized that its conservation principles ought to be adopted to create county energy districts, the purpose of which would be not only to conserve but to develop local renewable energy projects. The group called their incipient organization the Winneshiek Energy District and applied for and received federal stimulus funds.

The energy district's paid staff includes a Green Iowa AmeriCorps team, which conducts energy audits for households and provides residents with advice on lowering energy usage. The district also provides energy audits for farms and creates an energy plan for the farm, including both conservation and renewable sources. The success of the six-year-old Winneshiek Energy District's work has motivated adjacent counties to consider forming their own energy districts.

Of more far reaching consequence is an idea for a locally owned municipal utility, an idea that is widely shared in Decorah. Mosher and Grimstad are among the advocates of a municipal utility. "A local solar and wind powered utility," Grimstad wrote me, "would become a model for other municipal utilities, especially appealing to the 150 Iowa cities that have their own utilities."

Grimstad said that what he and other renewable advocates are doing, can only by done because there is considerable community support. Mosher and others share Grimstad's sentiment when he says, "I'm supposed to do these things. This is my job. I'm supposed to do this stuff."

*Keep Things Working, Cuban Style*
In his blog, independent journalist Frank Smyth reported in 1999 on the ingenuity that Cubans brought to the problem of keeping American cars running during the American boycott. While some Cuban car repairmen operate illegally to avoid paying taxes, ". . . [Delfín Matos] Ortíz operates legally and pays taxes. . . . As early as 1962 it was apparent to Ortíz, a former shipbuilder, that Cubans would have to fabricate their own engine parts to keep their American cars running. He spent six months painstakingly testing the metal composition of piston rings and taught himself how to make them. Today Ortíz, a great-grandfather, is still doing what he has done for decades, skillfully crafting piston rings for old American engines." Ortiz uses iron tubes, like the rusted ones he showed Smyth, and cuts them "into shiny new rings."

Writing for the *PBS Newshour,* Jenny Marder reported that "a washing machine welded to a boat propeller has become a makeshift fan. This kind of cobbled together contraption has become common in Cuba. So are stoves that run on diesel fuel from trucks, satellite dishes made of garbage can lids and lunch trays, and taxi signs consisting of old fuel canisters."

At the website, *http://www.lahabana.com/content/harlists-in-cuba/,* an anonymous writer and Harley lover, writes: "The Harley devotees fabricate their own parts or scavenge pieces from other motorcycles, cars, tractors, lawn mowers and even anti-tank guns." He quotes a Harley owner who told him, "We do whatever it takes to keep our Harleys on the road."

*Throwaway Society versus Salvage Society*

In a series of four dystopian novels, beginning with *A World Made by Hand,* James Howard Kuntsler presents a character who anticipated the collapse of American society and began amassing salvage. In Kuntzler's dystopic society, electric power is sporadic, industrial production has ceased and what's left of the United States lacks a common currency; therefore, the man in these novels who stockpiled goods and scrap of all kinds—and has the brutes to protect him—has power.

Let us be sure that our consumer throwaway society will not and cannot endure. We will, eventually, be forced to make do like the Cubans, and we will have to relearn old skills, thousands of skills that mechanization eradicated.

Suppose several cooperatives were created to begin stockpiling scrap as well as salvaging re-usable materials from building deconstructions, hauling the materials from outside the region to four or more great piles within the Driftless region: old cars, engines of all sorts, sheet metal, tires, fencing, plastic and metal pipe, wooden beams, roofing material, porch posts, jacks, hand tools . . . anything that can be re-used.

With furnaces to melt the scrap and with production tools and machinery to fabricate, much could be done. What would we want to fabricate? The answer would dictate the size of the furnaces and their costs. These are not only questions for a dystopian novel, but questions we could usefully ponder.

A society and culture that were truly sustainable would find a use for every bit of "waste," and would cease to manufacture items which do not biodegrade and cannot be recycled. If, like the founders of the New Alchemy Institute, we want to create an ark, we must mimic the cycles of the natural world. To do anything less is to continue our suicidal course.

# EPILOGUE

## PROVINCIAL HOPE

By the 1920s it was obvious to many observers that industrialization was homogenizing the United States. By the Great Depression, artists and writers were focusing more attention than ever on the American scene, depicting closely and with affection the life and folkways of their regions. Many of the artists and writers were perhaps recording regional life in the hopes of preserving memories of what had once existed; others were consciously trying to preserve what remained of them.

The wealth of what they created is, to my mind, the greatest treasure of American arts and letters, and when I want to illustrate regionalism I instinctively refer to three great painters: Thomas Hart Benton, Grant Wood, and John Stuart Curry.

*Regionalists and the Southern Agrarians*

In *Grant Wood* by James Dennis I learned about the Southern Agrarians, poets mostly, who had taught at Vanderbilt University and had decried the machine's intrusion into southern life. These men, including Robert Penn Warren, Donald Davidson, and John Crowe Ransom, wanted the South to turn its back on the North with its mechanization and to preserve its own agrarian roots. In 1930 they published a manifesto, *I'll Take my Stand.* Frank Owsley pretty well summed up the twelve writers' thoughts at the close of his own contribution: "This struggle between an agrarian and an industrial civilization, then, was the irrepressible conflict, the house divided against itself . . . The South had to be crushed out; it was in the way; it impeded the progress of the machine."

Wood and Benton's regionalist theories were stimulated by *I'll Take my Stand.* Aware of the power that art had for the revitalization of American culture, Wood wanted regional art centers established across the country. In her book

*Grant Wood: The Regionalist Vision*, Wanda Corn wrote that Wood's regionalism was a reaction to the cultural homogeneity threatening the nation. Wood, then, wanted diversity of folkways preserved, and saw art as a tool for that preservation. He hoped his own Stone City art colony, which ran for two summers in Stone City, Iowa in 1932 and 1933, would provide the model for other regional art centers, which would be instruments for cultural preservation.

Before ever learning of Wood's dream of regional art centers I had hoped to develop writing workshops in towns and cities throughout my region, workshops that would remain a vital part of the cultural and civic life of these towns. The point I am making here and elsewhere from my own regionalist experiments is that regionalism remains a vital possibility for decentralization, and that local art, literature and music are almost instinctively understood to be the best means available for developing regionalist sensibility. As I was later to find out, that was the belief of scores of other regionalists.

Cultural critic and generalist Lewis Mumford, whom I had personally known, had been a committed regionalist, spurred by the same concern that the Southern Agrarians and Wood had voiced: that the machine was producing a standardized and homogenized culture, and in the process was debasing humanity itself. In his regionalist years Mumford wrote: "At present . . . our metropolitanized populations throughout the world are both witless and wantless: true cannon-fodder, potential serfs for a new totalitarian feudalism . . ."

*Regionalist Artists and Writers of the 1920s and 1930s*
In the twenties Mumford had been part of a group called The Regional Planning Association of America. Mumford and his colleagues felt that the revitalization of the country depended upon decentralizing industry and banking, for the webs of

the power complex were and remain centered in urban areas. What Mumford and his friends envisioned was a limit to the growth of existing cities by infusing rural towns and areas with industry and the cultural institutions of the large city. It would mean creating what Mumford called regional cities. Beyond that, Mumford wanted regional cities to aggregate into regions bound together by ties of art and literature, language and folkways. Mumford's biographer Donald Miller says Mumford believed that these "tied people together more than social structures or ideology." Indeed, most regionalists, as creative writers, artists, and theorists, believed it too. B.A. Botkin, who compiled many folk literature anthologies, voiced the general notion when he wrote: ". . . the motifs, images, symbols, slogans, and idioms" of regionalism could bring about "regional, class, and other forms of collective consciousness."

Regionalists were clustered about the country, so naturally the centers of regionalism lay in the outlands themselves, in Taos and Santa Fe, in Lincoln and Iowa City, in Nashville and Chapel Hill, in Austin and Missoula. With the exception of Mumford (who lived in New York City until 1936 when he moved full time to a rural hamlet), the spokesmen for regionalism worked outside the centers of the power complex, the *loci* of the webs.

What all shared was a desire to bring into existence a quiltwork of cultures spanning the country. Which meant that regionalism was a theory of decentralization rooted in specific locality, and to the earth. But there was not always agreement on how to define a region. Howard Odum and Harry Estelle Moore began their book, *American Regionalism* (1938), with perhaps a score of definitions then in use. What bound this mix of regionalists together was the understanding that modern culture, thanks to mass communication, rapid transportation, and assembly line production, was producing a uniformity of experience and thought among

Americans. Above all, these modern instruments of trans-portation, production, and communication were producing a new psychology, a new individual: one without rootedness in place, without ties to the land, without community, one who acted from motives of expedience rather than from loyalty and truth. This was Mumford's "cannon-fodder." Thus none of the regionalists wanted a repetition of their own machine-dominated society, but rather a new civilization based upon a renewed humanism, animated by folkways and an art derived from local life. Art for all of them was crucial to the project, a conveyor of meanings.

*The 1940s: Regionalism Plays Out*

1936 marked the depth of the Depression, and it was a turning-point for regionalism. In painting, Wood, Benton, Curry, and their colleagues came under heavy attack from the advocates of abstractionism. For the theorists of regionalism— the Southern Agrarians, the members of the Regional Planning Association, for Howard Odum and B.A. Botkin—1936 was the year in which they realized that they had to enact their ideas or abandon their work.

The crisis of the Depression had created the possibility for reform, but by 1936 the possibility was fading. In that year the Southern Agrarians were breaking up, some having abandoned the cause. Also that year Odum, a professor at Chapel Hill, wrote: "For those who long easily 'to recapture the past' for Jeffersonian agrarianism, it must be pointed out that. . . the task is not so simple in the modern complex America." Sixty per cent of the population of his time, Odum wrote, lived in urban areas. By 1938 B.A. Botkin told Joseph Brandt, another regionalist, "Personally, I think the regionalism movement is almost played out."

The regionalists failed to implement their ideas because they had no method for doing so, and had no feeling for political realities. For most of them, writing was act enough:

most were academics and believed that education was sufficient to effect results.

With the Second World War, Americans began looking outward; the era of self-examination was over. With the Allied victory, America became the major power in global politics, while American industry began churning out products. The American citizen became a consumer.

## The Rebirth of Regionalism

In the years since the Second World War, books advocating the regionalization of the United States have appeared sporadically, including Joel Garreau's *The Nine Nations of North America* and Rexford Tugwell's profound work, *A Model Constitution for the United Republics of America.* Garreau divides North America into regions that are no more unanswered the question: Into how many republics shall we divide the United States.

But Tugwell's draft constitution, written and revised multiple times for The Center for the Study of Democratic Institutions, focuses on the failure of the Constitution to address multiple issues that the framers chose not to address. In so doing, the framers shifted important legislative decisions to the Supreme Court, decisions which (according to the Constitution itself) it should not make.

Now, in 2016, regionalism is no longer a side topic for café conversation. With the extreme fragility of society, the financial markets and the environment, people readily accept that regionalism is our only counter to globalism and the recreation of a human-centered society.

The Agricultural City is a regionalist vision that provides a model for a cooperative society in which meaningful, remunerative work is available to all. It advocates a culture rooted in the land and created with tools that enable a people to live harmoniously with the land.

Art and literature can help create this home for us by

fostering a regional consciousness, by offering dying rural towns an alternative to bitterness and passive acceptance of a System that works against them. Art and literature can inspire us to work towards the fulfillment of an economy and culture in which we are creators and not passive recipients. We need artists and writers who will help create the tone and energies from which a new society can emerge: we need artists who will bring the human figure back onto canvases and writers who will record the life of the everyday folk of their regions It is time to gather our energies and rebuild.

## END NOTES

CHAPTER ONE
*Mega-banks*
Dun & Bradstree; May 26, 2015t: http://bizmology.hoovers.
com/5-largest-us-banks-in-2015-who-is-winning/

*Seed Production & Concentration*
Food Democracy Now!: http://www.fooddemocracynow.
org/blog/2013/oct/4/the_gmo_seed_monopoly_fewer_
choices_higher_prices
According to *AgWeb*, "the 'big four' biotech seed companies
—Monsanto, DuPont/Pioneer, Syngenta and Dow AgroSci-
ences—own 80 percent of the U.S. corn market and 70 percent of the soybean business. They also control more than
half the world's seed supply."

*Beef Packing Concentration*
The Motley Fool: http://www.fool.com/investing/gener-
al/2015/09/17/yup-80-of-our-beef-comes-from-4-producers.
aspx

*Media Concentration*
Business Insider: http://www.businessinsider.com/these-6-
corporations-control-90-of-the-media-in-america-2012-6


CHAPTER TWO
*Infrastructure Rating*
"American Society of Engineers Report Card": http://www.
infrastructurereportcard.org/

*I-35 Bridge collapse*
https://en.wikipedia.org/wiki/I-35W_Mississippi_River_
bridge

*Flint, Michigan drinking water*
http://www.cnn.com/2016/03/04/us/flint-water-crisis-fast-facts/
and "EPA Flint Drinking Water Documents": https://
and www.epa.gov/flint/flint-drinking-water-documents

*Drone Strikes in Pakistan*
Center for Investigative Journalism: https://www.thebureau-
investigates.com/category/projects/drones/drones-graphs/
Watson Institute: http://watson.brown.edu/costsofwar/costs/
human/civilians/iraqi

*Agribusiness*
https://en.wikipedia.org/wiki/1993_Jack_in_the_Box_E._
coli_outbreak

*Banking & Finance*
Demos:http://www.demos.org/publication/brief-history-glass-steagall-act
Michael Lewis, *The Bog Short*. W.W. Norton, New York: 2010.

*Health Care*
*The Arizona Republic*:http://www.azcentral.com/story/news/local/arizona-investigations/2016/12/07/phoenix-veterans-hospital-gets-worst-va-ranking/95051764/
*Huffington Post*: http://www.huffingtonpost.com/art-levine/lt-general-coverup-kiley-_b_42596.html

*Education*
*Find Law*: http://education.findlaw.com/curriculum-stan-dards-school-funding/criticism-of-no-child-left-behind.html, and
*Education Week*: http://www.edweek.org/ew/section/multi-media/no-child-left-behind-overview-definition-summary.html

*Manufacturing*
*Investopia*:http://www.investopedia.com/slide-show/car-recalls/
and: http://www.investopedia.com/slide-show/car-recalls/

*Police Misconduct (Border Patrol)*
The Center for Invrstigative Reporting: http://bordercorruption.apps.cironline.org/ Ths site has links to numerous articles.

## CHAPTER FOUR

*Manufacturing Jobs Lost*: Economic Policy Institute: https://www.google.com/search?q=jobs+lost+during+Great+Recession&ie=utf-8&oe=utf-8#q=manufacturing+jobs+lost+between+2000+and+2004 A EPI paper also concludes" In short, the collapse in demand during the Great Recession and ensuing glacial recovery was responsible for most or all of the 1.4 million net manufacturing jobs lost between 2007 and 2014."
http://www.epi.org/publication/manufacturing-job-loss-trade-not-productivity-is-the-culprit/

*Social Security depletion*:
Government Accounting Office: https://www.ssa.gov/policy/docs/ssb/v70n3/v70n3p111.html

# BIBLIOGRAPHY

Alexander, Christopher. *A New Theory of Urban Design*. Oxford University Press, New York: 1987.

Anonymous. A *New Lease on Farmland: Assuring a Future for Farming in the Northeast*. (pamphlet) E.F. Schumacher Society, Great Barrington:1990.

Collum, Ed. "Community currencies in the United States." http://people.usm.maine.edu/collom/collom2005EPA.pdf

Corn, Wand. *Grant Wood: The Regionalist Vision*. Minneapolis Institute of Arts, Minneapolis: 1983.

Dorman, Robert L. *Revolt of the Provinces The Regionalist Movement in America*, 1920-1945. University of North Carolina Press, Chapel Hill: 1995.

Howard, Ebenezer. *Garden Cities of To-Morrow*. The M.I.T. Press, Cambridge: 1965.

Luccarelli, Mark. *Lewis Mumford and the Ecological Region: The Politics of Planning*. The Guilford Press, New York:1995.

Mumford, Lewis. *The Myth of the Machine: The Pentagon of Power*. Harcourt Brace Javanovitch, New York: 1970.

MacKaye, Benton. *The New Exploration: A Philosophy of Regional Planning*. Harcourt Brace and Company, New York: 1928.

Post, James E. Post & Fiona S. Wilson, "Too Good to Fail." Fall 2011. Stanford Social Innovation Review. http://ssir.org/articles/entry/toogood_to_fail

Ransom, John Crowe, et.al. *I'll Take My Stand:The South and the Agrarian Tradition*. Harper & Row, New York: 1937. The 12 essays by Southern agrarians capsulize all that need be said about the losses sustained by the industrialization of societies.

Restakis, John. *Humanizing the Economy: Co-operatives in the Age of Capital*. New Society Publishers, Gabriola Island, B.C. 2010.

Schumacher, E.F. *Small is Beautiful: Economics a if People Mattered*. Harper & Row, New York: 1973.

Schuman, Michael H. *Going Local: Creating Self-Reliant Communities in a Global Age*. Rutledge, New York: 2000.

Swann, Robert and Susan Witt. "Local Currencies for Sustain able Regional Economies." (pamphlet) E.F. Scchumacher Society, Great Barrington. 1995.

Taub, Richard P. *Doing Development in Arkansas*. University of Arkansas, Fayettevile: 2004.

Thompson, David. "Italy's Emilia Romagna." The Cooperative Grocer Network. 2004. http://www.grocer.coop/articles/italys-emilia-romagna

Truesdell, Mary Johnson & Cathy Johnson Noble. Hawarden's History. http://www.cityofhawarden.com/residentshawar dens-history/ *Independent Examiner*, Hawarden:2012

Tugwell, Rexford. *A Model Constitution for the United Republics of America*. Center for the Study of Democratic Institutions. Santa Barbara: 1970..

Witt, Susan and Robert Swann. "Land: Challenge and Opportunity." E.F. Schumacher Society, Great Barringto: 1995.

Wood, Grant."Revolt Against the City." Clio Press, Iowa City: 1935. This pamphlet was published under Wood's name but was written by Frank Luther Mott, who presumably based it on conversations with Wood or on notes Wood may have written.